BIRMINGHAM

in the age of the tram

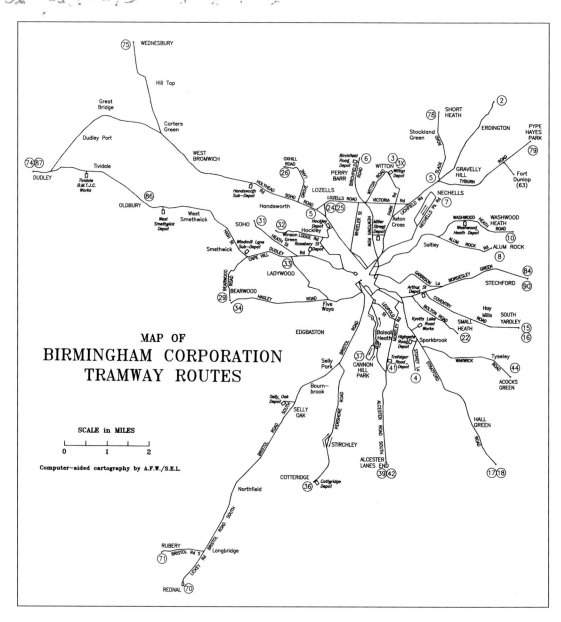

MAP OF
BIRMINGHAM CORPORATION
TRAMWAY ROUTES

SCALE in MILES

0   1   2

Computer—aided cartography by A.F.W./S.E.L.

Map of Birmingham Corporation tramway routes. This map shows the whole of the Birmingham tramway network, including the Coventry Road and Stratford Road routes in the south-east and the Ladywood, Lodge Road, Lozells, Perry Barr, Witton, Short Heath, Erdington, Pype Hayes, Washwood Heath and Alum Rock routes around the north of the city. It does not purport to show the system at any given date, being intended to locate each route to scale and place it in its geographical location. Only the route numbers of regular all-day tramcar services are shown. For detail of trackwork and locations of short-working turning points, see the definitive maps by J. C. Gillham, extracts of which are given in each chapter.

BIRMINGHAM
in the age of the tram
1933-53

The south-eastern
and northern routes

The city centre to South Yardley, Tyseley, Acocks Green, Ladywood, Lozells, Perry Barr, Witton, Short Heath, Erdington, Pype Hayes, Washwood Heath and Alum Rock

David Harvey

·THE NOSTALGIA OF BRITAIN·
from
The NOSTALGIA Collection

First published in 1993 as *A
Nostalgic Look at Birmingham
Trams 1933-1953 Volume 1*
Adapted and republished in this
format 2004

British Library Cataloguing in
Publication Data

A catalogue record for this book is
available from the British Library.

ISBN 1 85794 181 0

Silver Link Publishing Ltd
The Trundle
Ringstead Road
Great Addington
Kettering
Northants NN14 4BW

Tel/Fax: 01536 330588
email: sales@nostalgiacollection.com
Website: www.nostalgiacollection.com

Printed and bound in Great Britain

A Silver Link book
from
The NOSTALGIA *Collection*

ACKNOWLEDGEMENTS

The original book upon which this new edition is based would not have been possible but for the work of all the photographers who are credited within the main text. I am most grateful to the late W. A. Camwell, John Edgington, F. Lloyd Jones, the late L. W. Perkins, C. C. Thornburn and the late Ray Wilson for allowing so much of their respective photographic collections of the Birmingham municipal system to be used.

I am indebted to the late John Stanford of the Birmingham Transport Historical Group for all his comments, especially those regarding the dating of individual photographs, and to Richard Weaver for his valuable editing contribution.

I am also most grateful to Roger de Boer, whose knowledge of the local battery-electric dairy and dustcart fleets proved to be most useful.

A number of years ago I discovered the quite splendid photographs of the late Norman Glover. His pictures appear throughout this volume and his contributions in the form of personal reminiscences and his editing of the text have been extremely helpful.

My thanks also go to Stan Letts and Arthur Whitehouse for producing the general layout map of the Birmingham tram system, and to John Gillham for allowing me to use extracts from his most detailed Birmingham track layout maps.

Finally, as always, thanks to my wife, Diana, without whose hard work in typing the draft manuscript, critical comments, encouragement, patience and letting me off washing-up duties, this book would have been impossible.

CONTENTS

Car 613, a 1920 Brush bogie car, stands at the tram station shelters at Gravelly Hill on 10 September 1950, working the 5 service. This car was withdrawn prematurely in December 1952 after sustaining accident damage. Few places in Birmingham can have changed as much as this once important junction. Today the concrete pillars of the elevated M6 Gravelly Hill interchange, known colloquially as 'Spaghetti Junction', have completely altered this scene. The shops behind reveal much about life at this time. J. H. Barker, the butcher, is advertising bacon and meat through the rationing scheme that was still in force. Next door, Broad's Travel Bureau is promoting trips in the British Isles including holidays to Butlin's Holiday Villages and excursions to the Blackpool Illuminations. In the shop behind the tram shelter, television sets are being enthusiastically advertised, although the standard-sized 9-inch black and white models were still something of a novelty. *A. N. H. Glover*

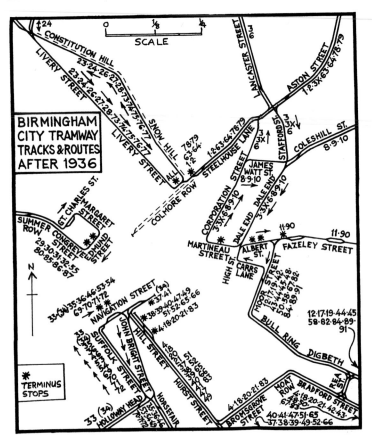

Left Birmingham City tramway tracks and routes after 1936. It can be seen that the city centre was never directly crossed by any route. This meant that tramcars transferring to another depot or going to Kyotts Lake Works frequently had to make circuitous journeys through the back streets around the perimeter of the city centre.

Termini in Birmingham city centre of the routes covered by this book.
A: Edmund Street (31, 32); E: Steelhouse Lane (1, 2, 63, 64, 78, 79); F: Martineau Street (3, 3X, 6, 7, 8, 9, 10); G: Dale End to Albert Street (13, 15, 17, 19, 44, 45, 56, 58, 82, 89, 91); K: Station Street (14, 16, 57); L: Station Street to Hill Street (18, 20, 21, 83); Q: Navigation Street (33, 34)

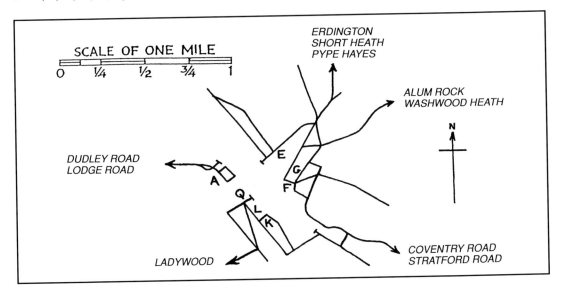

INTRODUCTION

The year 2003 marked the 50th anniversary of the final closure of the Birmingham Corporation tramway system. The Birmingham tramway fleet was well known for its high standard of mechanical maintenance and its immaculate dark blue and primrose paintwork. Unfortunately, to most people every Birmingham tram looked virtually the same. These tall, gaunt, even stately trams were part of the street scene in the city for 49 years, and perhaps it was only when they had gone that the public realised that part of their own lives had also disappeared.

The main problem with any history of Birmingham's municipal transport is the size of the operation – it was deceptively big. The city has a population that is still around the million mark and as a result the transport infrastructure has always had to be equally large. Birmingham had a total of 843 trams, a maximum number of 825 in service, 20 depots and yards, some 45 main routes and a total of 80.5 route miles. It was the largest 3ft 6in gauge system in the United Kingdom and was only exceeded in size by the tramways in London, Glasgow and Manchester.

Like other books in this series, this volume places the Birmingham tram in its social and historical context. Just as trams have been consigned to history, so have many of the streets and roads through which they ran. The photographs, nearly all of which had never been published before the original edition appeared in 1993, together with numerous new ones in this edition, capture moments in a period of time from about 1933 until 1953, and will bring back memories to those interested not just in Birmingham trams but also the street scenes and the many long-demolished buildings.

All cities are dynamic, in that they are constantly evolving, but the passing of the tramcar in Birmingham on 4 July 1953 corresponded with the start of one of the largest urban renewal programmes in postwar Britain. Put in simple terms, the trams' disappearance from the city was one of the first markers of dramatic change in Birmingham, which would eventually result in the partial pedestrianisation of the city centre, the extension of the central area along Broad Street to encompass the enormous investment of the International Conference Centre, the development of the 'Heartlands' project in Aston, Saltley and Bordesley, and the removal of vast tracts of old Victorian inner city housing. Perhaps, most contentiously, many of the small workshops and factories which enabled Birmingham to be known throughout the world as 'The City of a Thousand and One Trades' were also demolished. These areas were the domain of the tram, as were the inter-war suburbs that developed along many of the main arterial routes out of the city. Birmingham was at the forefront of the development of reserved track along the routes of suburbia, and throughout the 1920s new route extensions to serve the ever-enlarging suburban area were built.

As early as 1923 the standard outline of the totally enclosed Birmingham tramcar had evolved. The constant programme of rebuilding and remotoring was somewhat masked by the conservatively styled, rocker-panelled, hexagonal-dashed, wooden-framed, 16½-ton conveyances, which could sway along the Bristol Road South reserved track at speeds that left behind any competing bus.

By then, however, the future of the trams was already becoming more doubtful. Although two experimental lightweight trams were delivered in 1929 and 1930, three unremunerative routes had already been closed. Within two years the argument about the next generation of vehicle type, between the trolleybus and the oil-engined bus, had already gone against 'the silent service', and the development of the tramcar in Birmingham became superfluous.

This book looks at the Birmingham tramway routes that remained mainly on the northern and south-eastern sides of the city from about 1933, 20 years before the final abandonment. It examines each group of routes by undertaking a pictorial survey of trams in their street setting from the city to the outer terminus.

The routes covered are firstly those that fit

Car 357 of the 301 class turns into James Watt Street from Corporation Street on the Washwood Heath route. These UEC 52-seater trams were built in 1911, mounted on Preston 'flexible axle' 7ft 6in swing-yoke trucks, and fitted with Dick, Kerr DKBA 40hp motors; they were to give up to 39 years of service. Car 357 had been transferred from Coventry Road depot in October 1948 and was to become the official last car on the 10 route on the evening of Saturday 30 September 1950, being one of the cars that achieved about 1,170,000 miles in service. By this time they were some of the last open-balconied trams running on a narrow gauge system in the country. They were also unusual for Washwood Heath's allocation in that they were fitted with trolley-poles rather than bow collectors. *R. T. Wilson*

loosely into the geographical pattern and were abandoned earliest. This includes the Coventry Road services, which were the only ones to be replaced by trolleybuses after 1933, and the Stratford Road and Warwick Road routes. The routes to Lodge Road, Ladywood, Washwood Heath and Alum Rock, Perry Barr, Witton and Lozells, as well as the last group of services to be withdrawn, those to Short Heath, Pype Hayes and Erdington, are also covered in this volume. The aim has been to take the reader on a tram journey along each of the routes from its city terminus to its suburban destination.

COVENTRY ROAD

The Coventry Road routes shared with the Stratford Road services (see below) common city termini in High Street, for what became the 15 route, and Station Street, for the 16 route. They followed the same route out of the city as far as Bordesley, where the Coventry Road turned eastward underneath the Great Western Railway bridge and station. The development of the routes, however, followed a very different pattern from those of Stratford Road.

City of Birmingham Tramways Co (CBT) electric cars ran from the steam tram terminus at Small Heath Park across the city boundary at Hay Mills to Church Road, South Yardley, from 29 March 1904. CBT had run a steam tram service from the city centre to Small Heath Park from January 1886, but after reaching agreement with the Corporation, who relaid the track, a complete electric CBT service ran between Yardley and Station Street from 23 February 1905. This state of service was to last only until the CBT leases expired on New Year's Eve 1906, after which the service was jointly worked with the Corporation.

Coventry Road (alternatively known as Arthur Street) depot was opened on 24 November 1905 for the Stechford routes, and the operation of the Coventry Road service began as part of the joint operation on 1 January 1907. During 1911 negotiations with the CBT company to purchase all of its operations in the newly enlarged Birmingham area had taken place, and CBT operation on Coventry Road finished on 31 December of that year.

The Coventry Road route remained unaltered for the whole of its subsequent operational life. It was operated for most of that time by ex-Radial 71 Class cars or the smaller Brill trams from the 21 and 221 Classes.

After leaving Bordesley the cars climbed up Kingston Hill past Coventry Road, which at the time of opening had the largest capacity of any depot on the system, at 106 tramcars. At the junction of Cattell Road near the Birmingham City Football ground, the route turned right and passed through the linear Small Heath shopping centre which stretched over a half-mile section of the road. At the far end of these shops, at Charles Road opposite Small Heath Park, was the original steam tram terminus.

The route then descended past the last of the Victorian houses on Coventry Road whereupon it crossed the River Cole at Hay Mills. The flood plain of the river and its lower terraces were occupied by large factory units, and during the lifetime of the tram route the Singer Motor Works and the distant BSA factories could be seen. After the Hay Mills shops, the trams passed again into a residential area as they climbed through the erstwhile Yardley UDC to the terminus and CBT tram depot at Church Road opposite the Swan public house. Unusually for the Birmingham system, there was latterly a turning loop for the trams.

The only branch route was the Bolton Road 22 service which terminated in Waverley Road near the BSA factory. It, too, passed through an area of late-19th-century terraces before reaching the superior villas at the edge of Small Heath Park. The whole route was barely 1½ miles long and was never a financial success. It became the second route to be abandoned on 5 February 1930 and was replaced by one-man-operated buses.

By 1932 the Coventry Road services were regarded as something of a financial burden. After much deliberation, not helped by the 1933 Salter Report on the taxation of public service vehicles, which would have been enormously damaging to the trolleybus lobby, the Corporation opted for trolleybuses. A fleet of 50 Leyland TTBD2 six-wheelers with MCCW bodies was ordered, which at the time was the largest trolleybus contract ever placed.

The tram routes along Coventry Road were abandoned on Saturday 6 January 1934, and on the following morning Coventry Road depot was operating a mixed fleet, with the remaining trams being used on the Stechford service.

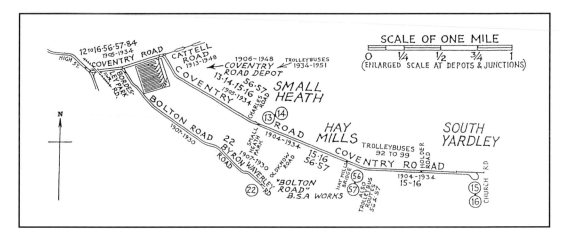

Above Coventry Road routes

Below Within a few years of entering service, the trams equipped with the small vestibule roller destination blinds had them replaced by the more cumbersome but more legible balcony 'flop-over' boards. United Electric Car Co (UEC) open-topper No 54, built in the spring of 1906 and fitted with Brill 21E 6-foot-long trucks, shows the driver-operated roller blind out of use, so this suggests it is about 1910 as this tram passes Small Heath Tavern on its way into the city. Corporation operation began along Coventry Road on 1 January 1907 as a joint operation with the previous sole operator, CBT. In the distance is the junction with Cattell Road, with the Greenway Arms public house and its well-known horse trough, which seemed to guard the bifurcating roads. This scene somehow encapsulates that Edwardian period, when every photograph seemed to be taken on a lovely sunny day, and women still wore long skirts but were liberated enough to ride the still fairly new safety cycles, as shown by the distant lady in the middle of the picture. The streets are lit with ornamental gas lights, and there is no motorised traffic, but the tarred roadway is well endowed with horse droppings – but ah, the rhubarb! *Birmingham Central Reference Library*

Above right Looking towards the city centre along Coventry Road in Small Heath in about 1910, the tower of the Wesleyan Chapel, built in 1876, dominates the skyline. The cyclist on the right is passing Grange Road, which in later years was used by the 16 and 17 bus routes as they returned from their termini in South Yardley. The shop on the corner of Grange Road, with its canvas sunblind drawn down, is a baker's, while next door, towards the entrance to the chapel, is a cycle repair shop.

On the left is Whitmore Street, and just beyond is Jenkins Street; between them is a shop whose stock is being cleared, and the fruit and greengrocer's shop owned by J. R. Taylor, who was still there 20 years later. Hidden because it is set back from the Coventry Road frontage, next to Taylor's shop is Small Heath Baptist Chapel, enabling the Nonconformists to 'do battle' across Coventry Road every Sunday. In the distance and travelling into the city are three trams, two with top-covers from the 71-220 class and an open-topper, car 269, one of the short, three-windowed UEC trams of May 1907, which were always referred to as 'The Brills', from the manufacturer of their 6-foot-long trucks. *Birmingham Central Reference Library*

Below right The CBT steam tram service was opened on 16 January 1886 as far as Dora Road, although within a year it was cut back to the coke yard just a few yards beyond Charles Road. The Corporation constructed a new electric tram track from Charles Road to the city boundary just under half a mile away under the terms of the CBT 1901 Parliamentary Act, and this was continued by the CBT company as far as The Swan at Yardley, as Yardley RDC waived its powers of purchase. The City of Birmingham Tramways Company opened its electric tram service between Charles Road and Yardley on 29 March 1904 using new Brush-bodied trams 181-188, which were mounted on a pair of Brush 4-foot-long D-type bogies. By early 1905 the eight trams were converted to run on Lycett & Conaty 8ft 6in Radial trucks after some unsatisfactory operations. CBT began to operate its electric trams from 23 February 1905 as a through service from Yardley to Station Street. Although the CBT lease within the city expired on 31 December 1906, when steam operation by the company ceased and

was replaced by Corporation electric trams, CBT continued to be the only operator on the section of the line between the city boundary at the River Cole in Hay Mills and Yardley. After that date there was a joint CBT/BCT service from 1 January 1907, whereupon the company only supplied eight trams on the route, with the balance of about 40 being supplied by the Corporation. When the city section of the lease expired, the Corporation took over the complete service on New Year's Day 1912.

Standing at the impressive gates of Victoria Park is CBT car 188, which appears to be still running on its original unsatisfactory bogies. With the steam tram track triangle entering the coke yard in the foreground, this picture dates from 1904, in the brief interregnum when this was where the steam and electric trams met. Victoria Park was on land given to Birmingham Corporation by Louisa Anne Ryland in 1876. This philanthropic lady also gave a donation of £6,000 towards the cost of landscaping the garden. It was opened as Small Heath Park in 1879, but needless to say was renamed in honour of the Queen's Golden Jubilee eight years later! *Commercial postcard*

Above In the early years of the 20th century Birmingham Corporation sanctioned the building of housing almost as far as Hay Barn Farm in the flood plain of the River Cole. By 1904 the side roads on the north side of Coventry Road had been laid out as far as Mansell Road, with the next road down, Aubrey Road, being laid out the following year, named after Aubrey John; as Lord Somerfield, his daughter married into the local Digby family, who had been the local landowners. The tram is CBT No 224, a Brush-built open-top 48-seater mounted on Brush-built Lycett & Conaty 8ft 6in trucks that entered service in late 1904. It is passing Tennyson Road at the eastern end of Victoria Park in about 1908, while in the distance, at Charles Road, is a top-covered BCT-owned 71 class car. *Commercial postcard*

Below Standing just below the terminal loop at the Yardley terminus is car 86, which is unloading its last passenger outside the Midland Bank before running around the loop at the junction of Church Road opposite The Swan Hotel. It will then return to High Street in the city centre. These 35hp cars originally had Mountain & Gibson Radial 8ft 6in trucks; they were designed to be self-centring after taking a curve, rather like a two-wheel bogie truck. Unfortunately, within a few years a combination of dust, mud and grease made the trucks' cornering characteristics somewhat idiosyncratic. The wheels would remain locked in the turning position or become rigid in the suspension. The result, as was found in Leeds with the later EMB Pivotal cars, was a very poor riding quality – it was bumpy and produced side oscillating motions at anything above 12mph. By the mid-1920s this car was one of the class to be re-equipped with Brush Peckham P35 trucks, and it remained in service until 30 September 1939, when it was sold for scrap after the Dudley Road abandonment. *S. J. Eades*

Above The opening of any electric tram route throughout the Edwardian period was a cause for celebration and civic ceremony, or at least, as is the case here, curiosity. On Tuesday 29 March 1904, with the almost new Swan public house in the background, the City of Birmingham Tramway Company began its operation of the ridiculously short route from the outer terminus at The Swan to Small Heath's Victoria Park. Because of leases, boundaries, territorial protection and what appears from a century later to be sheer bloody-mindedness, the operation of electric trams into Birmingham would take another nine months. Two of CBT's 181-188 class, the Brush open-toppers with short bogies, Nos 183 and 186, wait at the terminus on 23 February 1905 on the occasion of the beginning of the through running 'into the city over the boundary', while an electrical linesman is on top of the horse-drawn tower wagon at the very last traction pole on the route. The curved tracks on the right led to CBT's Yardley tram depot. Car 183 has the blind set ready for Birmingham, while 186 is loaded with top-deck passengers embarking for Yardley. But wait – they are already at Yardley, and if the destination blinds are not just set incorrectly, the trams are on the wrong tracks! *Author's collection*

Right The main stalwarts of the Coventry Road route in BCT days were the ex-Radial cars, and one of these, No 184, negotiates the terminal loop as well as, apparently, the shrubbery that dominated the centre of the island! Behind the tram, which is working on the 15 route to High Street, is The Swan public house on Sunday 8 October 1933. This elegant building replaced the old coaching inn of 1605 in 1898, and was designed in a mock-Elizabethan style; it dominated this important junction until 1967, when it was replaced with an anonymous structure whose

only claim to fame was that it contained the longest bar counter in the world. It too has since been demolished, lasting less than 30 years. *F. Lloyd*

STRATFORD ROAD

CBT steam trams had run since May 1885 as far as St John's Road, Sparkhill, and were extended by about 1 mile to College Road, Springfield, in 1900, the last steam tram extension built in Birmingham. Electric trams replaced the steam tram service on 1 January 1907. The Stratford Road route was prepared for electrification by CBT before its lease expired, and the steam trams finished without ceremony on New Year's Eve 1906.

The main Stratford Road electric tram service had two city termini, Station Street, beside New Street Station, and High Street. In 1915 the route from the former terminus was numbered 18 and the latter 17. Although the 17 moved to Dale End and finally to Albert Street, and the 18 moved round the corner to Hill Street, the basic concept that the routes served different areas of the city centre was maintained over the years.

On leaving the High Street area, the 17 tram route, together with the Coventry Road service 15 to Yardley, entered Moor Street and turned into the historical centre of Birmingham at the Bull Ring, whereupon it descended the steep hill into Digbeth.

The 18 route from Station Street went past the fruit and vegetable market in Moat Row and turned into Bradford Street, passing the city's main abattoir, before climbing up the hill to join the High Street service at Camp Hill.

Using the route common to the Coventry Road trams and one of the Stechford routes, as mentioned above, the trams passed through the mainly industrial areas of Deritend to the Coventry Road junction at Bordesley railway bridge. From here the Stratford Road cars, together with the Warwick Road 44 service from High Street, climbed up a steep rise to Camp Hill.

The cars then ran through the Victorian terraces and villas in Sparkbrook, travelling beneath the Midland Railway bridge at Henley Street, and immediately afterwards reached the junction with Kyotts Lake Road. Thereafter the Stoney Lane route branched off to the right at the start of the Sparkbrook shopping centre, and at the far end the Warwick Road route turned left, while the

main route carried on up the hill to the Sparkhill shops, passing the original steam tram terminus at St John's Road. The route reached the 1900 steam tram terminus at the limit of the pre-First World War housing at College Road, but it was extended into the open country at Fox Hollies Road in May 1914. On 2 April 1928 a final extension was made to the city boundary along a splendid piece of reserved track. This, in fact, proved to be the penultimate main-line route extension in the city's tramway system and served the huge inter-war suburban developments in Hall Green.

In later years Highgate Road depot at Sparkbrook operated some 40hp bogie cars from the 512 class along Stratford Road although continuing to use the earlier 21 Class, the ex-Radial four-wheelers and the 301 Class.

As already mentioned, the Stratford Road group of routes had one major branch along Warwick Road, which left Stratford Road at the Mermaid public house, Sparkbrook. It ran through the small 1880s shopping centre at Greet and climbed up to Tyseley, passing the entrance to the Great Western Railway's motive power depot. This marked the only shortworking on the route, numbered 91, the main 44 route carrying on to Acocks Green.

The original terminus was at Broad Lane; although the track along Warwick Road had been laid for about two years, because of track clearance problems the route was not opened until 2 February 1916. It was finally extended the last half-mile into Acocks Green in October 1922. The original terminus was also altered a few years later from adjacent to the Westley Road junction to the middle of the large traffic island in the centre of Acocks Green 'village'.

The second Stratford Road branch, along Stoney Lane, was opened at the same time as the conversion from steam tram operation in 1907. This was the 4 route and was one of the shortest branch routes on the Birmingham system, being barely three-quarters of a mile long.

Originally the Stratford Road routes were

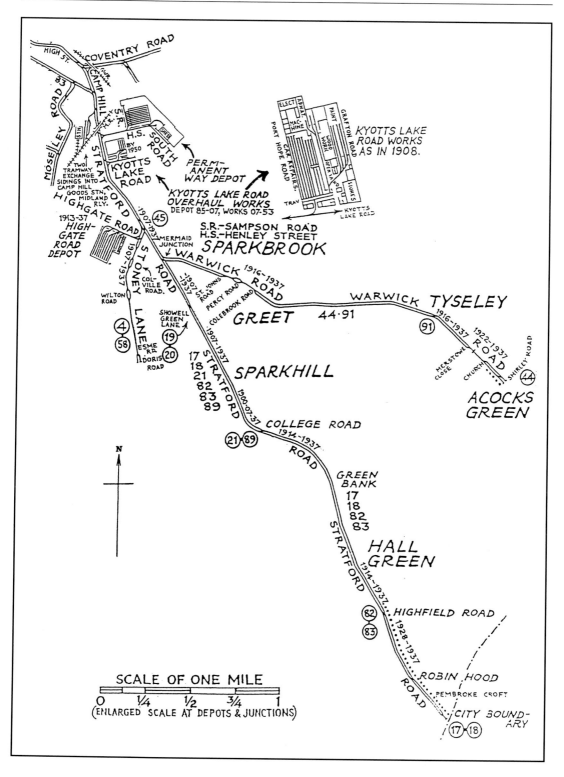

The Stratford Road and Warwick Road routes

partially operated from the old CBT headquarters at Kyotts Lake Road, but within a year of the introduction of electric tramcars 'The Lake' became the main repair works for the whole system. The Stratford Road and Stoney Lane routes were then operated by Coventry Road depot until Monday 24 November 1913. Upon the opening of Highgate Road depot, both services and the later Warwick Road route ran from this depot until the closure of the Stratford Road group when car 564 was finally pulled into the depot by enthusiasts in the early hours of 6 January 1937.

The Birmingham electric tramcar system suffered from having no direct route across the city centre and a scattering of termini just outside the main shopping area. Perhaps the most remote of these was Station Street, which was on the south side of New Street Station, where car 497 stands on the site of the triangular track junction opposite the Station Hotel. Just beyond the tram in the lower building are the premises of undertakers N. Wheatley & Sons. Car 497 was originally CBT car 236, built by the Brush Company of Loughborough in late 1904. It had been purchased in 1912 by BCT as one of the 61 trams taken over from CBT. When this photograph was taken in 1933, No 497 had been transformed from a green-and-cream-liveried open-topper into a 35hp tram with platform vestibules and top covers. It is on the 83 shortworking from Station Street to the Highfield Road junction on Stratford Road in Hall Green. Further down Station Street was the famous Birmingham Repertory Theatre, opened on 15 February 1913 with a production of Shakespeare's *Twelfth Night*. *J. Cull*

Confusingly, Camp Hill is a corruption of Kempe Hill, which was named after the Kempe family who were the landowners in the area in the late 15th century, and was not named after the camp set up there by Prince Rupert at Easter 1643 during a skirmish in the English Civil War. Over the succeeding years this historical quirk was largely forgotten, and when the area was developed after the opening of Camp Hill station by the Birmingham & Gloucester Railway in 1841, even the name of the Ship Hotel, which dated from the early 1850s, had the strange sub-title 'Prince Rupert's Headquarters – 1643'. In the year before the CBT steam tram service was extended to College Road, Springfield, in 1899, an almost new Kitson 'Improved' steam tram locomotive, No 90, shuffles towards the junction with Sandy Lane, on its way to the Sparkhill terminus, despite the destination board showing SPARKBROOK. *J. Whybrow*

Above In the early 1930s the abandonment of the Bolton Road and Hagley Road tram services meant that there was a surfeit of the larger, more powerful bogie cars. A policy of using them throughout the system was therefore introduced, which meant that the 'Brills' would be the prime candidates for early withdrawal. The 27 cars that had never received vestibules had gone by 1932, while car 36, seen here, was one of 60 trams to be withdrawn during the next year, in this case in June 1933. No 36 is working on a city-bound 44 service in Stratford Road, Sparkbrook, in about 1926. To the left, in the gap between Gillmore's Cash Drapery store and the Black Horse public house, is Kyotts Lake Road, where the Corporation tramcar works was located and where the last trams were broken up in August 1953. *R. T. Wilson*

Below There was frantic activity on the surviving CBT steam tram routes as, with the leases about to expire, the need for a seamless change to the Corporation's new electric tram service was deemed vital. Judging by the leaves on the trees, this work was begun in the early autumn of 1906, relegating the soon-to-be-replaced steam trams to single-line working, while the new electric rails were being laid. The navvies are working hard on this section of Stratford Road at the junction with Farm Road as the steam tram, appearing to be pushed by the Falcon-built steam locomotive, moves off towards Sparkbrook. *Birmingham Central Reference Library*

Above The prominent 120-foot-high west tower of St Agatha's Anglo-Catholic Church was built in 1901 as part of the church designed by W. H. Bidlake. Although Gothic in style, the architect managed to blend in a most unusual way some of the more suitable facets of the 'Arts and Crafts' movement, including the choice of red and white chequer brickwork and the pale cream brick interior. In the mid-1950s St Agatha's was nearly destroyed in an arson incident that destroyed the complete nave roof, but fortunately it was rebuilt. On the opposite side of Stratford Road were various blocks of two- and three-storey terrace blocks that had been built from as early as the 1850s, though the larger gabled properties were 20 years their junior. Car 110, one of the ubiquitous Radial-trucked trams built with top-covers by UEC, travels into the city on a briefly operated cross-city service from Sparkbrook to Washwood Heath in about 1910. *Author's collection*

Below The Stratford Road group of routes included a number that turned off the main route to Hall Green. The first turn was at Stoney Lane, where the 4 route, introduced on 1 January 1907, trundled barely half a mile to its first terminus at Esme Road. One of Highgate Road's four-wheel ex-Radial truck trams, No 213, stands in Stratford Road in 1937 having just turned out of Stoney Lane. Dominating this suburban junction in Sparkbrook is the large Baptist Church, built in 1879 when the distant three-storey terraces were quite new. In the row of shops this side of the church and Palmerston Road, the second belongs to George Green, who in 1937 was basically a seller of sheet music and a few 78s, but who by the late 1950s had become one of the best suburban record shops in the city. *L. W. Perkins*

Above The bustling Victorian shopping centre of Sparkbrook on Stratford Road was developed after the 1876 building bye-laws came into effect. The result was a swathe of terraced and tunnel-backed housing stretching from Highgate through Sparkbrook to Small Heath. UEC-built former Radial car No 163 stands in Stoney Lane just south-west of the junction with Stratford Road in late 1936, when working on the 4 route. The shops and houses were by then some 60 years old, and the days of the trams were already numbered. A 1936 Daimler COG5 flashes by along Stratford Road in the distance. These modern buses would sound the death-knell for the Stratford Road group of tram routes, the trams being unable to compete with them; they worked over the main road tram routes before branching off to the newer suburban developments not served by trams. By 5 January 1937 the trams had gone and the nearby Highgate Road depot was converted to bus operation. *R. T. Wilson*

Left UEC-bodied ex-Radial car 173 stands at the Doris Road terminus of the 4 route to Stoney Lane via Stratford Road, just beyond the Territorial Army Barracks. The original terminus was at Esme Road, but in about 1933 came one of the Birmingham tram system's great extensions! The Stoney Lane route was extended by 34 yards, by removing the last loop and terminal stub and replacing it with a double stub end. It is in one of these new track stubs on 4 January 1937 that No 173 awaits departure time on the Bundy Clock before embarking on its return journey to High Street. *R. Buckley*

Above Birmingham Central Tramways opened its route along Stratford Road in Sparkhill on 11 May 1885 as far as St John's Road, passing the Mermaid Inn at the junction with Warwick Road before climbing the quite steep hill to the terminus. The Stratford Road steam trams were the fourth to operate along a main road out of Birmingham, and here a BCT double-deck bogie steam tram trailer, No 35, built in 1885 as one of the 24-45 batch, is being pulled by a Kitson loco at about the time of the opening of the route. On the left, waiting outside the Mermaid, is a horse-bus working on the Warwick Road service. At this time the Mermaid was an important roadside inn, which had become a hostelry in 1751, though the Georgian facade of the building hid a property that pre-dated the start of the Civil War more than 100 years earlier. This building was replaced in 1895 by the present Victorian building, which,

after having been badly damaged in November 1940 in an air raid, was the centre of the Irish community in the area before being closed in the 1980s and most of the 1990s before its present-day revival. *Author's collection*

Below The busy suburb of Sparkbrook was, by the beginning of the 20th century, one of the most thriving parts of Birmingham, with an industrial area able to support a 'middle class' living in the large villa-type houses along Stratford Road and the adjoining Gladstone, Palmerston, Abbotsford and Anderton Roads. Even the more artisan 'tunnel-back' developments, built slightly later at the turn of the 1900s in Walford Road and the adjoining streets, reflected a prosperous area. At the centre of Sparkbrook were two shopping areas, the earlier one on the main road at Kyotts Lake Road and Farm Road, and the slightly later 1880s area on Stratford Road near Stoney Lane and the boundary with Sparkhill, which as part of Yardley UDC would not be incorporated into the city until 1911. UEC Radial tram No 118 passes the entrance to Warwick Road, with a horse-bus parked in front of the Mermaid Hotel on the right, having just crossed the boundary between Birmingham and Yardley about the time of this boundary change. Note that the horse, incidentally, is having his dinner! On this sunny day, the distant shops towards Walford Road have their canvas blinds extended as the tram begins its climb up the hill to St John's Road when working the S route in the summer of 1908. *Commercial postcard*

Above Standing at the St John's Road tram stop in 1907 on its way into the city is almost new car 144, having entered service only a few months earlier in 1906. Sparkhill had a population of only 5,000 in 1887, but 20 years later this had multiplied four times, and it had its own late-Victorian shopping centre at the top of the hill, beneath the spire of St John the Evangelist, consecrated in 1888, though Pevsner suggests that the spire was only added in 1905, or two years before UEC top-covered tram 144 stood outside Hodgett's bootmaker's shop. The church was given money for its upkeep and repair by the well-known Birmingham philanthropist Louisa Anne Ryland, who died the year after the church was consecrated. In the gap between the buildings on the right are the gates of the recently abandoned CBT steam tram coke yard. On the pavement, just behind the lady in the long black coat, the kerb still has not been made up where the tram tracks crossed the pavement. The following year a Salvation Army citadel was built on the site and is still there today. *Author's collection*

Below The only steam tram extension along Stratford Road was from St John's Road to College Road, Springfield, a distance of about a mile. This was opened on 5 May 1899 and was the last steam tram extension to open in Birmingham. Six bogie double-deckers, numbered 125-130, were bought from the Midland Railway Carriage & Wagon Company of Birmingham. These 70-seaters were single-ended, a practice not seen again in the city until the motorbus age. Almost new MRCW trailer car 128, on the S route, is about to meet an outbound steam tram and trailer as they pass Yardley UDC Council House, located in Sparkhill near Court Road. It was built in 1894 in red brick and terracotta with a large tower to the design of Arthur Harrison, and today serves as Sparkhill Library. *Author's collection*

Below The fourth shopping centre along Stratford Road was at Springfield, between Foremans Road and the River Cole bridge. It grew up in the late 1890s, and such was its rapid growth that it became the steam tram terminus in 1899, and remained the terminus of the new BCT electric tram route until it was extended to Highfield Road on 31 May 1914. BCT ordered 150 cars from Dick, Kerr & Co Ltd, which were delivered between August 1906 and March 1907 with UEC-built 52-seater bodies. Numbered 71-220, they were 16ft 0½in high, which enabled them to pass beneath the railway bridges in Stratford Road and Coventry Road. Because of this route availability, they quickly became the early 'backbone' of the fleet. In July 1911 UEC Radial car No 143 travels to the terminus, while just starting out for the city from this busy new

suburb is former open-top tram No 268, which had entered service in 1906 and had been one of the first trams of its class to have received a top cover earlier the same year. The trams are near the original electric tram terminus at College Road. *W. A. Camwell collection*

Bottom An immaculately painted car 571 climbs up the hill from Shaftesmoor Lane when working out of town on the 18 route in October 1936. This UEC-built 62-seater tram of 1914 mounted on Mountain & Gibson Burnley bogies had, during its life, three different motors, all 40hp Dick, Kerr pairs. The tram had its balconies enclosed in 1927 and was fitted at the same time with upholstered seats. It was one of 22 of the 512 class to operate out of Highgate Road depot, and except for its slow speed it entered the 1930s as an up-to-date, economical and efficient mover of passengers. Because of its low-horsepower motors, No 571 was transferred to the 'all-electric' Miller Street depot, rather than a high-speed air-brake one such as Selly Oak, and as such survived until the penultimate day of BCT tramway operation on Friday 3 July 1953. Following the tram is a Morris Twelve and an Austin Ten-Four, while one of the bus routes that overran the 'main-line' tram route before branching off, the 32 route, is being worked by an early Daimler COG5 of the AOB-registered series, distinguishable by its lack of a cream-painted waistrail. *W. A. Camwell*

Above The reserved track from south-east of Hamlet Road in Hall Green to the city boundary with Shirley was never really exploited by BCT, opening as the penultimate stretch of new track in the city, on 2 April 1928, and closing on 5 January 1937, although it has left the legacy of the wide central reservation on the main A34 Stratford Road. Towards the city the distant white buildings are the Art Deco Petersfield Court, which simply oozes 'Bauhaus' and is today one of the best buildings of its period to have survived in the city. Car 174 is working on a Hall Green-bound 18 service in the summer of 1936. This was one of Highgate Road depot's many UEC-bodied, ex-M&G Radial-trucked cars, which were re-trucked in the mid-1920s with 8ft 6in Brush Peckham P35 trucks. The car parked on the left is a Birmingham-registered 1936 Morris Eight. *W. A. Camwell*

Below Car 333 waits at the Hall Green terminus before working back to Walford Road. The Typhoo Tea advertisement on the side must have seemed a good slogan for the company, though not only would it fail to meet the present-day requirements of the Advertising Standards Agency, but could also be interpreted in exactly the opposite way to which it was meant! The tram is displaying the number 45 and is returning to Highgate Road depot, having worked along Stratford Road as far as Walford Road. The housing along Stratford Road near the city boundary was largely completed by 1925 and was served by the excellent tram service provided by the Corporation. Ironically, it wasn't this newest, outer section that was the problem, but the bus routes such as the 13, 24, 31 and 32 services, which all served municipal housing estates but took the revenue away from the trams.

This tram was built in 1911 by UEC and entered service in May of that year from Moseley Road depot, staying there until the 401 class, with the Spencer-Dawson oil and air brake, began working from that depot in the latter part of 1913. After a long period at, initially, Bournbrook depot and subsequently Selly Oak, No 333 was moved to Highgate Road in 1934 as one of 20 of the 301 class allocated there until the Stratford Road group of closures, when it began a somewhat nomadic life until settling down in 1942 to work the Bordesley Green service. Tram 333 was one of 50 of the class to be painted grey during the Second World War, and it survived until June 1948. *W. A. Camwell*

WARWICK ROAD AND ACOCKS GREEN

The Warwick Road route forked left at the Mermaid public house into Warwick Road, and replaced a horse-bus service that had ceased running approximately 14 years earlier. This was the second route to turn off the main Stratford Road tram 'network', and was the 44 service. It was first opened on 2 February 1916 and must have been a great relief to those who had lived in Greet and Tyseley and had to walk from the junction at Stratford Road. Similarly saved a long walk were the schoolchildren and staff of Yardley Grammar School, which occupied a site in Tyseley after 1904, as well as those railwaymen who worked at the Great Western Railway's Tyseley engine shed, which opened in June 1908.

On the right, guarding the entrance to Warwick Road, is one of the pair of silhouetted castellated towers belonging to the Mermaid public house. This impressive Victorian pub had been opened on the site of a Georgian inn in 1895. Above still open-vestibuled UEC-built top-covered tram No 189, on the 44 service, is the imposing Gothic-styled tower and spire of the Wesleyan Methodist Church on the corner of Medlicott Road, which would be destroyed in an air raid in November 1940. Next to the tram is a steam lorry with wisps of smoke issuing from its chimney. In later years one of the shops on the left would become well-known as the Mermaid Fish and Chip shop, a must for late-night cinema-goers emerging from the nearby Piccadilly picture house. *Commercial postcard*

Top Near the short-lived steam tram terminus at Greet Bridge over the River Cole, tramcar 452 is just about to pull away from the stop outside the Greet Inn public house on 5 May 1934. The steam trams operated by Birmingham Central Tramways first traversed Warwick Road on 16 November 1887 as a branch off the already well-established Stratford Road service. Unfortunately, the service was not a financial success and closed after little more than a year's operation, reverting to BCT's horse-buses once more, although Mr Thomas Lane also operated a horse-bus service until taken over by CBT in 1907. Car 452 was one of a pair of open-topped bogie cars taken over from CBT in 1912, having been that company's car 180. Used as a single-decker on an experimental trailer-towing service on the Washwood Heath route in 1917, this impressive five-bay tram was vestibuled and top-covered in early 1926 and allocated to Highgate Road depot, from where it was allocated to operate the 44 service. Beyond the tram, Warwick Road climbs up a quite steep hill, where a row of late Victorian terraces were reached only by precipitous flights of steps, just visible on the right-hand side of Warwick Road. Beyond a second hill crest was Tyseley railway station, opened on 1 October 1906, which gave the only real access to the length of Warwick Road between the Mermaid and Acocks Green village until the tram route opened. *F. J. Lloyd*

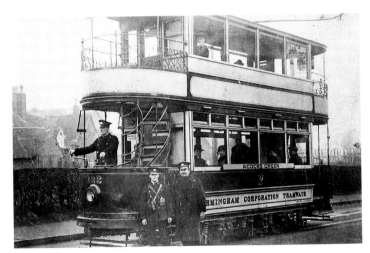

Middle The original terminus of the 44 Warwick Road route was about half a mile from Acocks Green at Broad Road. Car 132, one of the 71-220 class of UEC-bodied 52-seater trams with M&G 8ft 6in Radial trucks that had entered service in 1906, stands at this terminus in about 1918. The car, as yet unvestibuled, displays the 'Birmingham Corporation Tramways' lettering on the rocker panel and has a wooden slipboard showing the somewhat vague destination of 'Acocks Green' below the lower saloon side windows. *BCT*

Bottom The closure of the Stratford Road and Warwick Road service on the night of Tuesday 5 January 1937 led to the withdrawal of some 43 Brill-trucked tramcars. Car 69 approaches Acocks Green village on the rainy Sunday two days before the route abandonment. Just above the tram is the nave roof of St Mary the Virgin, the Parish Church of Acocks Green. The church was begun in 1864 and was intended to have a south-west steeple, but this was never built, leaving the church with a rather incomplete appearance. However, it's gem is its east window, which is by the Pre-Raphaelite painter Sir Edward Burne-Jones. The tram is working on the 45 shortworking service from Walford Road to Acocks Green. This route number was generally shown by trams on depot workings from Highgate Road depot; the destination blinds have already been rewound for the return journey to Sparkbrook. Car 69 had been fitted with the Maley track brake

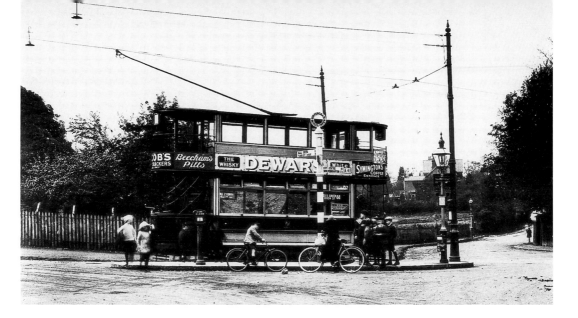

earlier in its life, but this was removed in October 1934. It was one of only nine members of these numerous little four-wheelers to be equipped for snowplough duties. The tram was broken up on 5 February 1937 at West Smethwick depot, just one month after its last official day on revenue service. *L. W. Perkins*

Above The Acocks Green route along Warwick Road to Broad Road was opened on 2 February 1916, being extended to Acocks Green 'village' in October 1922. Tram 245, a 1908 UEC former open-topper, stands at the still fairly new terminus on 3 May 1923. Acocks Green's Carnegie-funded library, the replacement New Inns public house and the Warwick Cinema had yet to be built, enabling the suburb to retain its rural appearance until the early 1930s. Off the picture, to the left of the tram, in Shirley Road, even at this late date, was one of the last working farms in the area. *Birmingham Public Works Department*

Below The Warwick Road 44 tram service holds the record for having the largest number of different termini in the shortest distance within Birmingham! Four termini were used in the 21 years of tramway operation, within 400 yards of each other. When the route was opened without ceremony on 2 February 1916, it was at a temporary terminus, at Broad Lane; the economic privations of the Great War made the necessary funding to widen the road in the centre of Acocks Green to carry the tram tracks unjustifiable. Consequently, the extension along Warwick Road into Acocks Green 'village' was not completed until 9 October 1922. Initially the trams stopped in Shirley Road just beyond the junction with Wesley Road, but after about five years the terminus was moved across the 'Green', almost in front of the Midland Bank Chambers in Warwick Road. In 1932 came the fourth terminus, which was located in the middle of the largest of the several new traffic islands, whose paving slabs had all but extinguished any trace of the greenery. Car 580, a UEC-bodied tram with M&G Burnley bogies built in early 1914, originally with open balconies, stands at this impressive final Acocks Green terminus on 3 January 1937. Behind the tram in Shirley Road are the mock-Elizabethan shop frontages built in a style typical of many early-20th-century shopping suburbs. *L. W. Perkins*

LADYWOOD

The Ladywood 33 route served the inner areas of Birmingham, passing through some of the oldest 19th-century back-to-back houses, as well as through areas of industry. The 2½-mile route, opened on 17 October 1906, took a somewhat devious route from Navigation Street in the city centre to the junction of Icknield Port Road and Dudley Road, and terminated only about 1½ miles from where it started. It was always operated by Rosebery Street depot, which was some half a mile citywards from the terminus at Dudley Road.

The original city terminus of the route was at the Queens Hotel end of Navigation Street, but in 1929 this was moved to where the Bristol Road group of routes began at the Suffolk Street end of the same street. From its opening until 1915 the route was identified on the trams by the stencil letter 'L'.

The cars left the city centre following the Bristol Road routes for the length of John Bright Street until, on reaching the Horsefair, they crossed the inbound Bristol Road cars and climbed Holloway Head and into Bath Row, passing some very poor-quality housing on the hill and St Thomas's Church; everything but the spire of this 18th-century church was destroyed in an air raid.

After passing Davenport's Brewery and the Queen's Hospital, the cars turned into Islington Row. The whole of this area was cleared in the 1950s and renamed Lee Bank, but for the latter years of the trams' involvement in public transport in the area, these were among the worst slum properties in the city.

At Five Ways the 34 route turned left and westwards towards the distant Kings Head

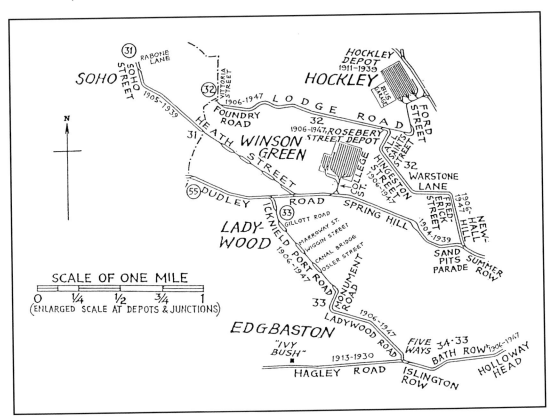

Ladywood and Lodge Road routes

terminus at Bearwood, but the Ladywood cars continued northwards past the Children's Hospital in Ladywood Road, again passing some early Victorian three-storey courtyard housing, before reaching Chamberlain Gardens at the corner of Monument Road. Here a remnant of the Regency housing of Edgbaston stood as a reminder of the time when nearby Ivy Bush was one of the most prosperous 19th-century areas in Birmingham.

The tram route turned right into Monument Road, then left into Icknield Port Road at the Municipal Bank. It then descended in a straight line into an area of factories for about a quarter of a mile, before beginning to climb again past factories towards some mid-19th-century three-storey terraces; this depressing landscape on the western side of the road successfully hid the tree-lined Rotton Park Reservoir. On this straight section of the route there were three passing loops, then at the terminus there was a section of double track that led into the left-handed curve that joined Dudley Road, but because of the narrowness of Icknield Port Road, cars stood in the single-track section. This of course meant that any outbound tram had to wait in the Gillott Road loop at the top of the Icknield Port Road hill until the terminus was cleared. Trams on depot workings from Rosebery Street could only reach Icknield Port Road by running beyond the junction on Dudley Road, then reversing to the start of the 33 route.

The route was originally operated by four-wheelers, but after 1926 Rosebery Street depot used the air-braked bogie trams from the 732 class. The service was withdrawn on 30 August 1947.

Having left Navigation Street, the 33 tram route traversed the length of the one-way John Bright Street before reaching the junction with the Horse Fair. The Ladywood-bound trams then turned right across the inbound Bristol Road and Pershore Road tram routes. These points are about to be approached by Brush-bodied car 747, one of the 63 hp air-braked trams of 1926, which will then begin the steep climb up Holloway Head. It is 1946 and the gap in the buildings in the distance towards Station Street is a grim memory of recent wartime bombing. Similarly, the buildings between the gap and the Paramount film distributors' office are boarded up and derelict. *J. S. Webb*

Above The pointsman has reset the junction in Suffolk Street under the watchful eye of the Inspector as the tram, Electro-Magnetic Brake Co (EMB) bogie air-brake car 735 of 1926, with a Brush 63-seat body, turns into Holloway Head on Sunday 31 March 1940, on a wrong-line working probably caused by track maintenance. Behind is car 837 on the 36 route to Cotteridge. Peterson's Rubber Co shop was destroyed in the bombing of 24-25 October 1940, one of the first serious nights of bombing that Birmingham suffered during the Second World War. *D. Clayton*

Below With the top of the distant Regency tower of St Thomas's Church peeping above it, tram 738 works its way out of town on the 33 route. Built by Brush in 1926, it has already been repainted in the '1946' livery, which was much simpler than the prewar lined-out version, having the rocker panels painted blue, with two blue bands between the decks; this was in common with the bus fleet livery. Only the prewar gilt fleet numbers were retained, and these were phased out during overhauls two years later. Following No 738 is another of Rosebery Street's EMB air-brake cars of the 732 class, which is also operating on the 33 route, while behind that is a Daimler COG5 bus, still with its radiator painted black after the war-time restrictions. On the left, the tram is passing the famous Queen's Hospital, better known as 'The Accident', which was built in 1840 by Bateman and Drury in a square-windowed architectural style that harked back to the Regency period. The grime-encrusted building on the extreme left is the 1873 extension. Today both buildings survive, having been converted into luxury flats. However, the three-storey early Victorian houses on the right were mercifully swept away when the south side of Bath Row was demolished as part of the Lee Bank Comprehensive Development Area, which was begun in 1952. *J. Whybrow*

Top Having reached Islington Row, the Ladywood route turned westwards towards Five Ways. Just before the First World War, men with straw boater hats stand on the platform of recently top-covered UEC car 254. Behind it, the second of the Brill-Maley trams, No 243, is coming into the city from Ladywood, with the far-off statue of Joseph Sturge in the centre of the Five Ways junction. On the right is William Street, and it was on this northern side of Islington Row that the retail premises were located, mainly in early Victorian properties. The houses on the left marked the eastern boundary of the Calthorpe Estate, which was maintained as an area renown for its 'upper class' Regency houses. Soon after the Great War, the 99-year leases on the Calthorpe Estate's properties in Islington Row came up for renewal and were either converted to offices or replaced with new buildings. Fortunately most of the rest of the Gough-Calthorpe family's development in Edgbaston survives in all its expensive, arboreal glory. *Commercial postcard*

Middle The Ladywood trams passed along Islington Row to the junction of Broad Street and Five Ways. On 28 August 1947 car 733, one of the 732-761 Class, crosses the junction in front of Lloyds Bank and the Art Deco shops at the top of Islington Row before passing into Ladywood Road. These bogie cars were synonymous with the 33 route and worked from Rosebery Street depot until it closed with the abandonment of the Ladywood route on 31 August 1947. *L. W. Perkins*

Bottom After passing the famous Birmingham Children's Hospital in Ladywood Road, the trams arrived at the junction with Monument Road, passing the now long since demolished premises of Thomas Furber & Sons, undertakers whose business had been established as long ago as 1868. Their premises, seen on the left of this 1947 view, lay opposite the Chamberlain Gardens recreation area, behind the tram. These were opened by the local Member of Parliament, Neville Chamberlain, on 28 June 1924. This photograph of car 754 was taken within a few months of the closure of the 33 route, and the last remnants of wartime restrictions are evident – the lamp-posts still have blackout markings and

there is a complete lack of cars, as petrol rationing is still in force. No 754 was uniquely fitted with a removable window at each balcony end in order to gain access to the trolley-pole. *J. S. Webb*

One of the ubiquitous Brush-bodied 732 class of air-braked cars, No 738, returns to the city centre on the 33 service. It is travelling along Monument Road and is about to pass the broken-down Morris Twelve that is parked on the other side of the road, then the row of shops with the recently 'demobbed' Austin 10hp light utility van. Mr Smith's grocery shop on the corner of Hyde Road has long since disappeared, but on this sunny day in the early summer of 1947 that was many years away. To the right of the tram, just before the shops, is the parish church of Ladywood, St John's, built in 1854. *J. H. Taylforth collection*

On a dark, dismal day in 1947, car 740 has just turned out of Monument Road into Icknield Port Road. The Birmingham Municipal Bank to the right of the tram was typical of the smaller branches established in the years after the First World War, in this case opened by the Lord Mayor, a Miss Williams, on 14 June 1924. The West Bromwich-registered two-door Morris Eight saloon was almost new when this view was taken. The queue of intending passengers spilling into the roadway would not be possible with today's traffic. *Author's collection*

'Post it to Vernons, the pools you can trust' sits a little uncomfortably on the advertising hoarding next to the entreaties to join the Territorial Army. Car 733, one of the EMB air-brake cars, rattles through the first of the three passing loops in Icknield Port Road, near the Henry Wiggins wire factory, on its way to the terminus in August 1947. Most people seem oblivious to the tram, still in its prewar livery, the advertisements and the nearly new Morris Eight four-door saloon. *W. A. Camwell*

The middle passing loop on the 33 route in Icknield Port Road was at the Belle View public house. This Ansell's house has survived, but virtually all the houses have since been demolished; the large factory complexes behind the two trams are also still there today. On the right is car 747, outward bound from the city centre to the terminus about half a mile away, passing inbound car 740 during the last few weeks of operation. This latter tram is in the prewar lined-out livery, the somewhat faded grandeur of which does not do it justice when compared to the recently repainted 747. *J. S. Webb*

Above The Dick, Kerr DK30/1L 63hp motors of 738, one of the 732-761 class, were wasted in the confines of deepest Victorian Ladywood. It is 1947 and the tram has been repainted into the simpler postwar livery, though still retaining the prewar fleet numbers. Some of the three-storey terrace houses in Icknield Port Road had, by this time, been converted to shops, but even the sunshine could do no more than temporarily brighten up the already run-down cobbled street. *W. A. Camwell*

Below The wartime Bedford OYD 5-ton lorry has just turned into Icknield Port Road from Dudley Road and is approaching the tramcar, which is waiting at its terminus opposite the somewhat uncared-for Bundy Clock. The condition of some of these three-storey properties was already quite appalling, but it would be more than 30 years before they would be replaced. The only building that survives today is the Wheatsheaf public house on the corner with Dudley Road. It is 1946 and bogie car No 736 is still in its prewar livery. At the end of tramcar operation from its depot at Rosebery Street, this tram would be transferred to Selly Oak, where its 63hp motors would at last be able to be used to some advantage. *Burrows Brothers*

LODGE ROAD

Competing with the famous 'Chinese Railway' routes in Balsall Heath for being the most tortuous on the BCT system, Lodge Road also had the added problem of being one of the hilliest. The nature of the route, and the fact that a fatal accident occurred on 1 October 1907 in Warstone Lane involving car 22, resulted in Lodge Road always being worked by the smallest four-wheel trams in the fleet. A total of 54 cars from the 21-70 and 221-300 classes were equipped with the Maley track brake in 1909 and 1910 as a response to the accident, and some were specifically allocated to the Lodge Road route. In 1926 15 of these small Brill-Maley cars were fitted with new bow collectors, and up to 18 trams in all were fitted with this method of current collection exclusively for the Lodge Road route.

The route itself (see the map on page 28) started beneath the pedestrian bridge in Edmund Street between the Council House and its later Edwardian extension. On leaving the terminus, the route turned into Congreve Street and continued into Summer Row, where it met the inbound cars. These turned into Great Charles Street and unloaded in Edmund Street, effectively giving all the Dudley Road group of routes a turning loop around the city's administrative buildings.

The outbound cars followed the Dudley Road routes as far as Newhall Hill, where they turned right up the steep hill into the Jewellery Quarter. After passing along Frederick Street, with its

The bases of the lamp-posts, the kerbstones and the fenders of the trams are painted white as part of the early wartime blackout measures. It is 30 September 1939, the last day of operation of the Dudley Road routes, which is ironic as the condition of the distant tram, working on the 85 service to Spon Lane, appears to be much better than the nearer car, No 260. Yet while the newer four-bay car would be broken up within a few months, car 260 would survive the war, being finally broken up in July 1947, some four months after its final withdrawal, when it closed the Lodge Road service. Standing under the bridge, built in 1913 to link the Museum and Art Gallery to the Council House extension, car 260 waits in Edmund Street at the loading shelters before embarking on the 16-minute journey to Foundry Road, where it will unload its passengers beneath a less auspicious bridge. *J. S. Webb*

19th-century workshops and converted houses, the tram route turned left at the Chamberlain Clock and descended Warstone Hill, passing Key Hill Cemetery, one of the oldest burial grounds in Birmingham. At the bottom of the hill the cars passed the famous Birmingham Mint before crossing Icknield Street and the Inner Circle bus route. The route then climbed Hingeston Street and turned right over the GWR railway line near Hockley Goods Station.

The 32 route then turned left and climbed Lodge Road, with terraced houses to the right and the mid-19th-century All Saints Hospital and Winson Green Prison to the left. On reaching Winson Green Road, the trams crossed the Outer Circle bus route and descended Foundry Road, passing an area of late-Victorian tunnel-back terraces before reaching the terminus.

The Lodge Road route was unique in the Birmingham tram system in that it started and finished beneath bridges – at the outer terminus this was a railway bridge at the city boundary. The trams reversed at a terminal stub cross-over opposite the Railway Inn.

The Lodge Road route should have been withdrawn at the same time as the rest of the Dudley Road tram services, but was reprieved for the duration of the Second World War, and was not abandoned until 29 March 1947.

Below On a wet day in January 1947, car 262, fitted with a snowplough, follows an FHA-registered BMMO FEDD bus fitted with an as yet unrebuilt Brush body along Congreve Street. The tram is passing the long-forgotten White Horse Hotel; this stood opposite the rear of the Council House extension of 1913, which contained the offices of the City Transport Department. Both the tram and the Midland Red bus are travelling towards Summer Row, where the hoardings on the left mark the location of Saturday Bridge, which crossed the Newhall branch of the

Birmingham Canal Navigation. Just visible in the road opposite W. & J. George's premises are the inbound tram tracks turning into Great Charles Street, which took the Dudley Road group of tram routes, as well as the Lodge Road service, 'around the block' of the Council House extension into Margaret Street to the terminus in Edmund Street. *National Tramway Museum*

Above right Turning from Summer Row into Great Charles Street on its way into the city is car 259. This was

one of 17 Brill-Maley-equipped UEC-built trams built between 1905 and 1906, and retained to operated on the Lodge Road route. Their short 6-foot wheelbase made them eminently suitable for the tortuous tight turns on the route, especially in their re-motored 40hp form. Although their withdrawal was delayed by the Second World War, the trams of this class allocated to the Lodge Road route were among the first on the system to be equipped with the Fischer bow collector, which was subsequently modified by the fitting of the self-lubricating Rowland skate. Apparently towering over the junction with Great Charles Street, although it was only five storeys high, is the large premises occupied on the upper floors by W. & J. George, manufacturers of chemical and scientific apparatus. On the right, in Great Charles Street, is a Ford Model Y Fordor saloon, which in 1934, when new, cost £125. *J. H. Taylforth collection*

Below Once over the crest of Saturday Bridge across the Birmingham & Fazeley Canal in Summer Row, the outbound route descended considerably towards The Parade. Saturday Bridge was so called because it was here that on Saturdays the canal workers and the bargees were paid their weekly wages. Parked on the left is a Worcestershire-registered Morris Eight of December 1934, while above it and to the left of the tram is the Council House extension. Beyond that, exemplifying the Victorian civic pride in the town of Birmingham, the impressive 'Big Brum' clock tower sits on the top of Yeoville Thomason's City Museum and Art Gallery, which was completed in 1885. Car 222, working on the 32 service to Lodge Road, sits on the crest of the hill with daylight just visible between the top of the cobbled road surface and the Brill 21E trucks. *R. V. Dudley collection*

Above Two contrasting types of tramcar allocated to Rosebery Street depot pass each other at the bottom of The Parade at the height of the Munich Crisis on Tuesday 27 September 1938. No 262, one of the small UEC-bodied 48-seater trams fitted with a 6-foot-long Brill 21E truck, has just left the turn from Newhall Hill into The Parade while working on the 32 service into the city centre. These trams were equipped with the Maley track brake especially for the Lodge Road route. On the right, totally enclosed bogie tram 635 is a Brush-bodied 62-seater mounted on Brush-built Burnley bogies and latterly equipped with English Electric DK30/1L 63hp motors. To the right of No 635 is the impressive classically styled entrance porch of Hoyle, Robson Barnett & Co, paint manufacturers. On the left behind the railings is the local sub-Post Office and its attendant Gilbert Scott-designed cast-iron telephone box. *W. A. Camwell*

Below The tortuous curves of the Lodge Road route were always a feature and led to its nickname of 'The Dipper'. The 32 route was also quite hilly, the steepest part being Newhall Hill, which led from the Dudley Road routes at Sandpits Parade up to Warstone Lane clock at the heart of the Jewellery Quarter in Hockley. The lantern-lit King Edward VI public house on the left and the late Victorian Buckingham Buildings factory on the right guard the entrance to Newhall Hill as Brill-Maley car 49 starts to ascend in this early postwar view. *G. F. Skipp*

Above At the top of Warstone Lane is the famous Birmingham Jewellery Quarter. This area has been developed continuously since the 18th century and is a mixture of impressive purpose-built works and converted houses with rear workshops down entries and narrow passages. The centre of the Jewellery Quarter is the Chamberlain Clock at the junction of Frederick Street and Vyse Street with Warstone Lane. It is a cast-iron memorial marking Joseph Chamberlain's visit to South Africa in 1903; unveiled by his wife, Mary, on 30 January 1904, it was restored in the late 1980s to its ornately painted best. Car 222 approaches the clock before turning left from Frederick Street into Warstone Lane. It will then descend the hill carefully, as this was the site of the 1 October 1907 accident when car 22, basically of the same type as 222 but in original open-top condition, overturned with the loss of two lives. *Newman College collection*

Below Looking down Warstone Lane from the Chamberlain Clock, on the right, adjacent to the planted, but as yet not in use bus stop, is the Midland Bank on the corner of Vyse Street, which leads into the heart of the Jewellery Quarter. The bank opened in 1892, and over the front door is a statue and stone carving associated with Henry Vyse's coat of arms. The tall building behind the inbound car 262 in Warstone Lane stands on the corner of Tenby Street North, and was occupied by a variety of manufacturing jewellers, a spoon-maker and an electro-plate manufacturer. In early 1947, not long before the abandonment on 29 March, car 262 has climbed the hill in Warstone Lane having just passed the entrance to Key Hill Cemetery, one of the oldest in Birmingham. About to pass this tram is car 50, still painted in the wartime grey livery in which it would be withdrawn. *National Tramway Museum*

Above Again in early 1947, UEC-bodied three-bay car 61 has travelled down Warstone Lane, having left behind the entrance to Key Hill Cemetery. The isolated two-storey building on the right-hand side of the hill is the Red Lion public house. At the bottom of Warstone Lane is the junction with Icknield Street on the left and Carver Street to the right, with the dining rooms of Mr Thornton at 108 and 109. The tram tracks in the foreground will take the tram across Icknield Street and into Hingeston Street, then on towards the Lodge Road terminus at Foundry Road. *J. S. Webb*

Below The trams descended the 1-in-17 hill in Hingeston Street from the Hockley Goods Station at All Saints Road. Occupying the corner of Hingeston Street and Icknield Street was the Royal Mint public house, owned by the Aston-based Atkinson's Brewery and managed briefly by the parents of Birmingham-born actor Tony Britton. Icknield Street followed the line of the Roman Ryknield Street, which ran from the south to Wall, the legion's staging post of Letocetum, near Lichfield. Unusually, the premises in Icknield Street were numbered consecutively down the east side, then back up the west side. Brill-Maley car 244 waits at the Belisha crossing in Hingeston Street on 20 April 1939. *L. W. Perkins*

The sharp curves of the 32 route can be appreciated in this prewar view of car 61 in Lodge Road on 29 July 1939. The abandoned single line in the foreground had been the link between Rosebery Street and Hockley tram depots, but the latter had been converted to bus operation on 1 April 1939. The tram is passing a small row of shops; glimpsed beyond it is a Bradford's electric bread van, while on the right is a Fordson van owned by the famous butchers Marsh & Baxter. An advertisement for Kodak film on the left belies the fact that this was only five weeks before the outbreak of the Second World War, and that soon such luxuries would be a thing of the past. *H. B. Priestley*

Top As it climbed Lodge Road, the 32 route passed a series of fairly grim reminders of Victorian social history. The first was the City Fever Hospital, established in 1875 so that more smallpox and scarlet fever victims could be isolated. The trams then passed the architecturally impressive but sobering Borough Lunatic Asylum; built in the style of a Tudor mansion and opened in 1850, it is now All Saints Hospital. At the top of Lodge Road was the gaol, built like a toy fortress, castellated and round-arched, which later became HM Prison Winson Green. It was designed in 1849 by D. R. Hill, the same architect who was responsible for the asylum. Car 53 lets off passengers near the prison in 1946. It will next cross Winson Green Road and go down Foundry Road to the terminus less than a quarter of a mile away. *J. S. Webb*

Middle The terminus of the 32 service was in Foundry Road. The route always displayed 'LODGE ROAD' on the destination boxes, but the tram terminus and pick-up point was outside the Railway Inn. In fact, this public house was on the corner of Wellington Street and Vittoria Street, and it is in the latter that car 255 is standing. The 32 service was therefore serving the Lodge Road area, but the terminus of the route was neither where the tram stated it was going nor where it has always been assumed the terminus was located! In 1944, still fitted with wartime headlight masks and white-painted fenders, behind No 255 is car 61 of the same type. *National Tramway Museum*

Bottom The Hillman car is parked outside the Railway Inn as, perhaps, its driver enjoys the delights of the locally brewed Mitchells & Butlers beer. Car 61 stands beneath the railway embankment next to the Bundy Clock, which recorded departure times on a card roll when the driver turned a key beneath the clock face. This view, taken on a rather overcast 29 July 1939, shows evocatively the simple stub terminal line in this rather depressing industrial environment. The advertising hoardings extol the virtues of healthy living by drinking milk, smoking Wills's 'Star' cigarettes - only 9d for 20 - and 'Persil whiteness'. *H. B. Priestley*

WASHWOOD HEATH

The 4½-mile run to Washwood Heath on the 10 route to some extent epitomised the variations in Birmingham's urban landscape during its journey via Saltley to The Fox and Goose. The route was opened on 2 May 1907 and the service was initially operated by 71 class cars and some of the smaller open-topped 21 and 221 classes from Washwood Heath depot.

The 10 route, which was lettered 'W' until 1915, started in Martineau Street with the Alum Rock, Nechells, Witton and Perry Barr routes. Martineau Street was probably the city terminus nearest to the main shopping streets, and the routes that used it gave their passengers certain advantages regarding walking distances, although this was somewhat negated by the terminus not having any covered tram stops.

On leaving the third loading stand from the top of Martineau Street, the trams turned into Corporation Street passing en route some of the largest and most popular shops in the city centre. They then passed the Old Square, where Newbury's department store stood, later replaced by Lewis's, then proceeded along Corporation Street until they reached the junction with John Watt Street. Here, in later years, because of problems with trams with trolley-poles at junctions designed for bow-collector operation, 301 class cars would have to be de-poled before proceeding out of the city beyond this point.

The whole of Corporation Street became the subject of a police review of traffic congestion in the city centre in 1931, which resulted in the development of Birmingham's famous (or infamous) one-way system, which started in 1933. The result, as far as all the Martineau Street routes, including the Washwood Heath services, were concerned, was that from Bull Street to the Old Square the trams ran against the one-way system on their outward journey.

On reaching the bottom of James Watt Street, the trams turned across the inbound trams from Witton coming along Stafford Street. The Washwood Heath services then ran through Ashted, a once prosperous Regency area, whose early wealth had been overtaken by the rapid mid-19th-century expansion of industrial Birmingham: Coleshill Street, Prospect Row and Ashted Row were a mixture of terraces, courtyards and some of the first municipal housing built in the 19th century. From Great Francis Street to Saltley Road were houses that would be swept away under one of Birmingham's first comprehensive urban renewal plans.

At Saltley Road the landscape changed dramatically as the Rea Valley was crossed. Here were numerous railway sidings, the Birmingham & Warwick Junction Canal and a mixture of small workshops and large factories, all bound together by the permeating smell from Saltley Gas Works. After crossing Saltley Viaduct over the flat flood plain, High Street, Saltley, and the Gate public house were reached.

The Gate marked the junction where the Alum Rock route carried straight on through the main Saltley shopping centre. The 10 route, however, turned left into Washwood Heath Road and climbed through a residential area as far as the tram depot just after a small shopping area at Aston Church Road. The route then dropped down a steep hill to Ward End Park and the Morris Motor works before curving round the edge of the park to the original terminus at Sladefield Road, in another shopping area.

A route extension left Sladefield Road as the 9 shortworking when, on 20 December 1913, the new section, three-quarters of a mile long, was opened to The Fox and Goose public house at Bromford Lane. This enabled the route to serve the proposed housing developments near the new terminus, most of which were not in fact built until after the First World War. An unusual feature of part of this last extension was the side reservation from Chetwynd Road to the terminus.

This route and that to Alum Rock were selected for conversion to bow-collector operation after September 1928 when the 762-811 class of EMB air-brake cars was allocated to Washwood Heath. These trams ran the Washwood Heath route, supported by a few older four-wheelers, until the trams were replaced by buses on 1 October 1950.

It is worth noting that, like Coventry Road

depot, Washwood Heath also operated trolleybuses and motor buses; in this case they were for the Nechells route, which had been the first tram route to be replaced by trolleybuses in Britain, in November 1922. The trolleybuses ran from the depot to Bloomsbury Street, Saltley, using the positive tram overhead and a skate on the rail for the return current. On 1 October 1940 the route was abandoned because these 'skate-operated' depot journeys produced a good deal of arcing and a lot of sparking, which was not considered conducive to a good blackout, especially during air raids.

Below Routes through Saltley to Washwood Heath and Alum Rock

Above right The 50 Brush-bodied EMB air brake tramcars of the 762 class were all assembled at Moseley Road depot and entered service between September 1928 and February 1929. When car 770 was photographed in 1934 in Dale End on the 10 route, it was not yet six years old. The care taken in the appearance of the tram, which was also apparent in the bus fleet, can be seen by the reflection of the sunshine on the cream paintwork below the front balcony and on the highly varnished deep, dark blue. The tram has unloaded most of its passengers and is passing A. D. Wimbush's bakery and café, which was situated almost on the corner of Albert Street. The distant shop with the round-topped signboard belongs to the chemist's chain owned by Hedges, which was still there in 1950 when car 766 was photographed in the next but one picture. *R. T. Wilson*

Below right At the very end of tramway operation at Washwood Heath, some of the last 'new' trams to be transferred to the depot were some of the few remaining four-wheel, open-balcony trams from the 301 class. Belying its 39 years, a well maintained car 383, working on the 10 service, stands in Dale End on Friday 18 August 1950. In front of it is exposed-radiator Crossley DD42/7 No 2352 (JOJ 352), which entered service on 1 February 1950 and is working on the 33 route to Finchley Road, Kingstanding. Both vehicles will turn right into Martineau Street after waiting for the man with the overloaded handcart to clear the junction. *Author's collection*

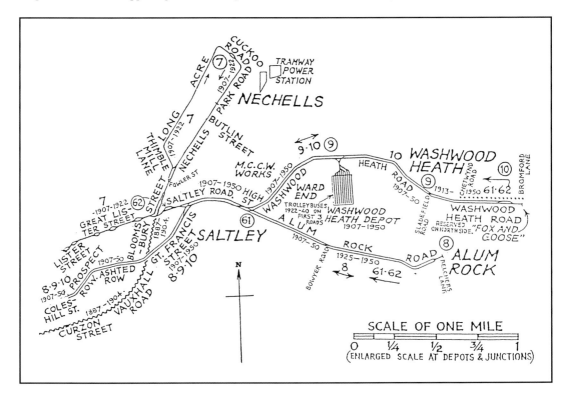

Above Turning from Dale End into Martineau Street, in front of the small island that contained a gentlemen's subterranean toilet, is car 766. Delivered new to Washwood Heath depot in 1928 to replace that depot's allocation of ex-Radial cars, it was one of the Brush-built air brake cars that ran with bow collectors until the closure of the Washwood Heath route on 30 September 1950. In common with the other 48 cars that survived the Second World War, it was transferred to Selly Oak depot. The destination number blind has an unusually large '0' as part of the route number '10'. Tram 766 was withdrawn about two months before the rest of the class, in May 1952, because of a defective truck. One of Perry Barr garage's Leyland 'Titan' PD2/1s of the 1656-1755 class, built in 1948 with Brush bodies, is following the tram round into Martineau Street on the 33 bus route from Kingstanding. *Author's collection*

Below This view of a really bustling scene in April 1949 shows, besides car 769 on the 10 route, a newly repainted Leyland TTBD2 six-wheel trolleybus turning out of Carrs Lane. It is passing the News Theatre that was opened on 18 January 1932 by Neville Chamberlain, who was at that time Chancellor of the Exchequer. The Waverley Hotel

beside it was an Ansell's public house on the small triangular site formed by High Street, New Meeting Street and Albert Street, and has the impedimenta of clock and lantern-style light adorning its facade; in front of it stands a policeman on point duty. Albert Street, into which the trolleybus will turn, contained the terminus of some of the Moseley Road trams, Stechford trams and the Coventry Road trolleybuses, as well as Birmingham's famous 'Beehive' store. To the left of the tram, at this six-way junction, is the lower part of Bull Street with the tobacconist on the rounded corner. *F. Lloyd Jones*

Above right By mid-1950 the Alum Rock routes were being prepared for abandonment. They were a mixture of reserved track that involved running on one side of the road! In Martineau Street and throughout the city centre, kerb loading was standard practice. Car 773, one of the 1928 EMB air brake cars, is working the Alum Rock 8 route, and is standing behind bus 1737, a 1948 Leyland 'Titan' PD2/1 with a Brush H30/24R body. This is working the 39 route to Witton via Aston Cross and Villa Park, home of Aston Villa FC. In the distance, in Corporation Street, is a Park Royal-bodied wartime bus. *A. B. Cross*

Below On turning right from Martineau Street, the 8 and 10 tram routes travelled along Corporation Street, but on reaching Lewis's department store and Bull Street, the trams actually went against the one-way traffic flow as far as Old Square. Passing hatmakers G. A. Dunn & Co, which occupied the first three shops after Lower Bull Street, is EMB air brake car 801. The Brush bodies fitted to these tramcars were built with eight windows per upper saloon side; these were aesthetically unpleasing, but were fitted so that each passenger could 'control their own ventilation'. The tram has three of these windows boarded up after losing the window glass in the air-raid that damaged many of the trams in Washwood Heath depot when it was hit by a bomb on 9 April 1941. The car was repaired with painted hardboard in the windows and was pressed back into service within days of the bombing. *Author's collection*

Above The open-balcony 301 class cars allocated to Washwood Heath were only ever equipped with trolley-poles. As a result they could not go straight on up Alum Rock Road because the overhead was set up for bow-collector-fitted trams, and were therefore restricted to the 10 route. Even this caused problems, as at James Watt Street, where the conductor had to re-wire the trolley-pole in order to leave Corporation Street. Tramcar 344 begins to turn across Corporation Street into James Watt Street on 12 July 1950, while five-month-old exposed-radiatored Crossley DD42/7 bus No 2356 (JOJ 356) travels into the city on the 5 route from Perry Common. The tall white building in the background on the far side of Old Square is the impressive seven-storey Lewis's building of 1929, designed by G. de C. Fraser. *G. F. Douglas*

Below James Watt Street hardly exists today, with only a short length of the buildings at the top of the hill on the right still remaining. A rather shabby car 769 working the 8 route to Alum Rock descends the hill to the junction with Stafford Street and Dale End on a warm summer's day, 7 June 1950. It carries a Barber's Teas advertisement on the balcony panel; Barber's was a local firm, established in 1797, and based in Pershore Street. Their quarter-pound packets of tea contained picture cards, which were more collectable than the tea! Barber's were taken over by Twinings in about 1961. *F. Lloyd*

Today, Coleshill Street, where the two air brake cars Nos 781 and 804 are standing, is but a memory. Parts of the campus of Aston University now cover this site, while the Victorian shops and warehouses have all been razed to the ground, including, on the right, Thomas Padmore's billiard table manufacturing premises, as well as Samuel James at No 6, who was a dealer in earthenware, china and glass and who also had one of the most visible of all gable-end advertisements in Birmingham. Occupying many of the units along Coleshill Street was Gaskell & Chambers, who as well as being brass founders also supplied public houses with bar pump engines. Car 781 is coming into the city on the 10 service during September 1950, while similar Brush-bodied EMB bogie car 804 travels in the opposite direction to Washwood Heath. *J. S. Webb*

Above Where Coleshill Street met the triangular junction with A. B. Row to the right and Prospect Row to the left, there was a rather splendid decorated cast-iron urinal. Bow-collector bogie car 807 is coming into the city from Washwood Heath in 1949. On the left, in the shadows, a woman pushes her baby in a heavy-looking pram, passed the rather domestic-looking premises of H. Thompson, manufacturing chemist. In the distance are the gaunt, skeletal remains of a building in Ashted Row that had been destroyed in the Second World War. A. B. Row not only had the shortest street name, but was politically and geographically important as it marked the old boundary between the parishes of Aston and Birmingham. Prospect Row was so named because it gave fine views over the Georgian-inspired Vauxhall Gardens, which closed on 17 September 1850. *F. Lloyd Jones*

Below Ashted Row was a very prosperous area in Birmingham, having been laid out by Dr John Ash, who had been partly responsible for the building of the General Hospital in 1779. From his acquired wealth, Ash had purchased part of the Holte family's estate in Duddeston, but not long after announcing his intention to develop the area, he sold the land to John Brooke, a lawyer, and moved to London. Brooke was by contemporary accounts not a particularly pleasant person, but he did name his newly acquired land 'Ashtead' after Dr Ash. By the mid-1850s the nearby Vauxhall Gardens had succumbed to the ever-increasing urban sprawl, but the once elegant Georgian houses in Ashted Row, on the left behind the tramcar, managed to retain their higher status, being occupied by doctors until well into the 1950s. As late as 1956, between Henry Street and Bloomsbury Street these splendid three-storey residences housed some eight physicians. On a bleak-looking day in September 1950, car 796 unloads outside the three-storey Ashted Terrace and the low extension of the Ashted Tavern public house. *J. S. Webb*

Above The corner of Ashted Row and Great Francis Street marked the change from the older and originally prosperous early-19th-century area and the later mid-Victorian artisans' terraces that continued into neighbouring Saltley and Duddeston. Car 762, the first of the 1928 Brush-bodied EMB Burnley bogie air-brake cars, stands on the outward-bound curve of Ashted Row on its way to Alum Rock. The soldier who is striding purposefully across the road between the lorry and the rear of the tram is a reminder that the hostilities of the Second World War had not long been over and that National Service in the armed forces was in operation. *F. Lloyd Jones*

Below Car 344 is travelling along Great Francis Street towards the city centre on the 10 route, and is approaching the turn into Ashted Row, having passed the Junction public house. This pub was owned by Atkinson's Brewery, which supplied its beer from the nearby Aston Park Brewery. Atkinson's was taken over by Mitchells & Butlers in 1959; the pub itself fell victim in 1950 to part of the largest urban redevelopment programme in the country. This erased the previous street pattern and replaced it in 1952 with three brick-built 12-storey flats, High, Home and Queens Tower, which have unofficially become known as 'The Dreadnoughts'. Just to the left of the pub is Bloomsbury Street, part of the old CBT horse-tram route to Nechells. Following the open-balcony tram is car 774, which although equipped as a totally enclosed bogie car, is only 17 years newer than the smart, but somewhat antiquated four-wheeler. *W. A. Camwell*

Above Great Francis Street was never particularly pleasant, backing on to the old LNWR railway line and in site and smell of the numerous gas works in Saltley. When it rained, however, it did look particularly grim, as here in September 1950. All the tramcars operating on the 8 and 10 services were based at Washwood Heath depot, which, despite having all 50 of the 762 class of EMB Brush-bodied air brake cars of 1928, had, prior to the summer of 1940, an allocation of about 56 trams, as well as the Nechells trolleybuses. From 1948 until the end of tram operation from Washwood Heath, there were always between four and six of the 301 class open-balcony four-

wheelers allocated to the depot. They were usually used for peak-period shortworkings, although they were to be found on the 10 route as tramcar availability was reduced prior to the closure. Car 381, on its way into the city centre, has just passed over the crossover that enabled the 62 route shortworking to return to the outer terminus at Washwood Heath. *J. S. Webb*

Below The Victorian terraces of Great Francis Street and Saltley Road lacked everything except utilitarianism, and were to be demolished in the early 1950s as part of the Nechells Park Comprehensive Development area. They

stood in the shadow of the ex-LNWR line to the North West, which opened as the Grand Junction Railway on 4 July 1837 and was the first line built in Birmingham. Behind the bridge are the gas holders at Saltley Gas Works. Car 344 is having its pole turned after working the 62 route from Washwood Heath on 4 September 1950. Although the four-wheeler is in apparently good condition, it would be withdrawn on 30 September, to be broken up at Witton depot two months later. Beyond, bogie car 782 waits for the older tram to return to the out-of-city line. The rear of a passing prewar Daimler COG5 bus, probably working in from Glebe Farm, can be seen in Saltley Road. *T. J. Edgington*

Above This is the same junction looking from Saltley Road towards the LNWR railway line and Saltley Viaduct beyond on 29 October 1950. This scene had looked very much like this for many years, but it was to change the following day when the Washwood Heath-Alum Rock tram services were converted to buses. The distant 'new look'-fronted Crossley DD42/7 bus is only a few months old and is working the 14 route from Glebe Farm. One of this class, No 2489 (JOJ 489), has been preserved in full working order since 1969. The track in the foreground is the disconnected access for depot workings for the Nechells 7 route trams, which had been the first BCT abandonment in 1922. The tracks remained, however, because of the necessity to use a skate return on the replacement trolleybus journeys from Bloomsbury Street to Washwood Heath depot. This lasted until the arcing from the skate on depot journeys resulted in the 'temporary' withdrawal of the route on 1 October 1940 – under the ARP lighting restrictions it was thought that the arcing would make the trolleybuses a target for Luftwaffe pilots, but it is debatable if this was true! *D. R. Harvey collection*

Below Saltley was incorporated into Birmingham in 1891, but during the previous 30 years sewage works and latterly gas works had been built in the area alongside the Midland Railway's line to Leicester. From then until the 1960s, the pungent, sickening smell of gas permeated Saltley and the surrounding Victorian tunnel-back housing. The strange fact was that, statistically, there was a smaller incidence of colds and chest infections in the area than anywhere else in the city! With the gas works in the background, a Corporation bus working on the Inner Circle service turns into Saltley Place in September 1950. This was unusual for the 8 route, on which the attractive Leyland-bodied Leyland 'Titan' TD6cs were not common performers. In Saltley Road, giving way to the bus, is Brush-bodied air brake car 770. It is working on the 10 route and will shortly accelerate over Saltley Viaduct on its way to the Gate junction. The rectangular tram stops will shortly be taken down and be replaced by bus stops, but the existing bus stop, on the right at least, was actually originally for the 14 bus route and has been in use since the introduction of services to Lea Hall on 13 December 1933. *R. T. Wilson*

Above The little girl on her tricycle being shepherded by her father might be envious of the young woman cyclist bouncing over the cobbles of Saltley Viaduct in the shadow of car 779, which has rumbled its way past Saltley railway station and is on its way to the Gate junction. This is just visible in the distance, where a Daimler COG5 on the Inner Circle 8 service is turning out of Adderley Road. To the left of the viaduct is the headquarters and works of Metropolitan-Cammell, where the body of the bus would have been constructed. *F. Lloyd Jones*

Below Looking in the opposite direction in late September 1950, the bus stop at Crawford Street on the east end of Saltley Viaduct will soon be getting extra customers as the tram services are in their last week of operation. The notice of abandonment in the upper saloon balcony window of car 763 means that within days Birmingham will only have two groups of tram routes left, one on the high-speed track along Bristol Road and the other via Aston to serve the Erdington area. Car 763 is travelling towards the city over Saltley Viaduct with the gas-holders towering over the industrial landscape. *R. T. Wilson*

Above The Gate at Saltley was a well-known public house that dated from 1873, although it had replaced a much older turnpike hostelry. This was where Washwood Heath Road swung to the left and Alum Rock Road went straight on, and was the first main suburban shopping centre on the Washwood Heath tram routes. The wide-ranging shops were in High Street, in the foreground, along Alum Rock Road, which was traversed by the 8 tram route, as well as in the first hundred yards or so of Washwood Heath Road. The four trams around this busy junction are all members of the 50-strong 762 class, which entered service in September 1928. The totally enclosed 62-seater bodies were built by the Brush Company and had eight windows on each side of the upper saloon. They were mounted on EMB Burnley bogies and were fitted with 63hp motors and EMB air brakes. The 10 route was particularly known for its fast running times, and in order to speed services further, these trams were fitted with a modified Fischer bow collector, which also had the advantage of relieving conductors of their trolley duties at the outer termini. Car 786, still with the prewar gilt fleet numbers, turns into High Street on its way into the city on the 10 route, having just been passed on the parallel outbound curve into Washwood Heath Road by car 770, with the simplified fleet numbers that were first used in 1946. This tram is being followed by a Morris-Commercial CV11 ambulance, which although first registered in September 1947, was only taken over by Birmingham City Council in 1948 when four different ambulance providers were amalgamated and operated as a separate division of the City's Fire Brigade. In the shadows, outside the Gate public house, is similar car 784 on the 8 route, which has given way to the pair of trams on the 10 service. *G. F. Douglas*

Above The River Rea flows eastwards through Saltley in a wide and flat valley. In 1858 the first sewage filtration works was built on the Rea flood plain, but with the population of Birmingham growing rapidly, by the 1860s the 140-acre plant was reduced to a 'sodden morass' with the most 'pestilent stench'. In 1884 the newly formed Tame & Rea District Drainage Board opened up a new sewage farm and the healthy state of the area was once more restored. The 1876 building byelaws had prevented any further back-to-back housing developments, but by the late 1880s terraced through houses and tunnel-backs were being built, opening up the Washwood Heath area beyond the new sewage works, which had been common land until enclosure in 1817. Car 798 passes the earliest of these Victorian developments at Havelock Road on its way along Washwood Heath Road to Ward End. The car is equipped with a trolley-pole, which had been fitted in the summer of 1950 when the car had been in Kyotts Lake Road Works in preparation for its use from Selly Oak depot. *R. T. Wilson*

Left The conductress braces herself before the tram starts off from the stop outside Washwood Heath depot, although perhaps, at the end of her 'turn', she would have preferred to have been in the Cross Guns public house next door. Car 784 is on the shortworking 62 service, which is going into the city but will work to the Saltley Road junction with Great Francis Street. There it will use the reverse crossover, where car 381 was seen earlier. Just visible on the roof of the tram are the wooden weather rails, fitted to prevent a situation when the trams were new whereby the guttering next to the bow-collector might become 'live'. In the background, through the trees, is the spire of St Mark's Church, consecrated in 1899. *R. Knibbs*

Below Washwood Heath depot was opened to traffic on 2 May 1907 with a capacity for 66 trams on 11 depot roads, together with whatever space was available in the yard. The introduction of the Nechells trolleybuses on 27 November 1922 saw the depot housing on average about 16 trolleybuses until their 'temporary' withdrawal on 20 September 1940, when it was used solely for tramcars, remaining open despite being bombed on 9 April 1941. Buses were introduced on a regular basis in August 1946 when some of Liverpool Street's services were transferred, but after the abandonment of the Washwood Heath group of tram services on 1 October 1950, buses 'ruled the roost'. The garage was finally closed by Travel West Midlands in 1998. In the spring of 1950, just before open-balcony four-wheeler tramcar 382 was transferred to Miller Street depot, five bogie cars stand at the entrance to the depot. Coincidentally, these include car 800 on the extreme left, which was destined to be the last service car to Cotteridge, and, next to it, car 777, which officially closed the Bristol Road services, both events occurring late in the evening of 5 July 1952. Roads 7, 8 and 9, where car 381 is standing, are where the trolleybuses were garaged. *G. F. Douglas*

Above One of the last 26 open-balconied four-wheel trams in service was car 381. It was transferred from Miller Street to Washwood Heath depot on 10 September 1949 and ran until the day before the Washwood Heath closure. These 301 class cars were built to a height of 15ft 7½in, which enabled them to have a universal route availability and to some extent made them the most useful cars on the system. No 381 is standing with car 768 in Washwood Heath Road just below the depot entrance and near the Leigh Road junction, which led to the Midland Railway Carriage & Wagon Company factory; this eventually became the Metropolitan-Cammell bus-building works, which finally closed in late 1989. *R. T. Wilson*

Below As Birmingham spread out into the countryside in the late 19th century, so the need for public recreational open space became more important. In 1903 the city purchased some 53 acres of land in Ward End, which included the rather splendid Georgian home of Birmingham's first historian, William Hutton, who, in 1781, had written *The History of Birmingham.* A large ornamental boating pool, fed by a natural spring, was built in 1909, while an aviary and a winter garden were added just prior to the First World War. This open space became Ward End Park, on whose wall on the right two prospective Midland Red passengers are waiting. Opposite them people are queuing to board car 773. The stop here at Drews Lane had become one of the busiest in the city as it catered for the workforce of the Wolseley Motors factory which, by 1950, had become Morris Motors Ltd. *R. T. Wilson*

Above On a rainy day in late September 1950, just before the closure of the tram routes operated by Washwood Heath depot, EMB air brake bogie car 769 travels down the hill towards Ward End Park on its way into the city on the 10 route. By this date the tram is equipped with a trolley-pole instead of the bow collector usually associated with these two routes. These were fitted in preparation for these 762 class trams to operate their final 20 months of service running from Selly Oak depot on the Bristol Road routes, where bow collectors were not used. The tram has just passed over the crossover at Sladefield Road, which was where the 9 route shortworking terminated. A woman on the right looks on disconsolately as the tram departs in the wrong direction leaving her to get even wetter as she waits at the replacement bus stop for a Fox and Goose-bound tram. On the left, outside Coles double-fronted drapery shop at Nos 605 and 607 Washwood Heath Road and Toy's butchers shop next door, which was the final shop in the row, is a Ford Prefect E93A four-door saloon – when new in 1947 this would have cost £352 – while partly hidden by a cyclist is a wonderfully stylish Jaguar 1½ litre. *J. S. Webb*

Below Beyond Ward End Park, Washwood Heath Road rises steadily uphill and passes through the tree-lined pre-First World War shopping centre of Ward End. Car 786 is travelling out of the city towards the terminus at The Fox and Goose public house about half a mile away. The tram has passed Sladefield Road on the right and is approaching the next tram stop at Asquith Road, which marked the end of the shopping row on the left. Between Sladefield Road and the Standard 8hp is a Belisha beacon with its studded road crossing of a type introduced in 1934; during the 12 months following the abandonment of the Washwood Heath tram services, Belisha beacons throughout the country would be converted to 'zebra crossings', with black and white road stripes. *R. T. Wilson*

Above The final approach to the Washwood Heath terminus at The Fox and Goose public house was on a 600-yard stretch of reserved track from Chetwynd Road along the north side of Washwood Heath Road. The houses on the side of the reservation date from the mid-1920s, while those on the right in this view just predate the First World War. Fischer bow collector-equipped No 769 has just left the street track and crossed the road to enter the reserved track. Noticeable in this view, silhouetted against the sky, is the shaped piece of wood fitted to the edge of the roof of the tram in place of the metal roof guttering; apparently, when new the bow collector fixing brackets could make the guttering become live. This car was modified at Washwood Heath in October 1928 to eliminate this problem, but cars 774-811 were modified by the Brush Company before delivery. In the background is open balcony 301 class car 357 which, unlike 769, is carrying the simpler postwar style of number. *W. A. Camwell*

Below The short length of reserved track at the terminus served as a useful parking place for trams when Washwood Heath depot was being converted into a bus garage in the summer of 1950. At evenings and weekends cars were stabled on both tracks and the service curtailed at a temporary crossover a short distance from the terminus. Cars 768 and 763 are at the front of three cars parked on the in-bound track some weeks before the final abandonment. The reserved track was built in anticipation of a dual-carriageway scheme, which had to wait until the late 1970s before it came to fruition. In the background, a service car waits opposite the Beaufort Cinema as a Midland Red SOS FEDD-type double-decker comes into Birmingham on the 160 service. *R. B. Parr*

Top The trams that were replaced at Washwood Heath depot by the 762 class with bow collectors were some 22 of the little Brill 21E-trucked cars and 34 of the 71 class. Car 217, one of the latter, stands at the original terminus outside The Fox and Goose public house at the junction with Bromford Lane. The route was extended from Sladefield Road to this new terminus on 20 December 1913 and remained here until well after car 217 was transferred to West Smethwick depot. The Fox and Goose was rebuilt from a 'mish-mash' of early-19th-century buildings on the same site; the replacement building was designed by Holland W. Hobbiss in a magnificently flamboyant Tudor style and was opened in 1913 during the same year that the trams got to Bromford Lane. *Commercial postcard*

Middle The magnificent mock-Tudor Beaufort Cinema at the Washwood Heath terminus was opened on 4 August 1929 and was fitted with a two-manual, eight-unit Compton organ. This instrument was played by Reginald New who, in the 1930s, did radio broadcasts for the BBC from the Beaufort. The instrument was eventually removed to the EMI studio at St John's Wood, London, in 1937, and the cinema itself was finally closed on 19 August 1978. Car 787, seen on 17 July 1949, is unusually carrying an advertisement for the firm of E. R. Green, which was based in High Street, Kings Heath, and was a well-known ladies' clothier. The Beaufort is showing the film *The Street with No Name* starring Mark Stevens, an American leading man who usually appeared in routine B movies. Also appearing in this film, made in 1948, was Richard Widmark; it was his third major film before he moved on to star in films such as *The Alamo* and *Madigan*. *O. M. Capes*

Bottom At 1.40pm on 2 September 1950 two buses pass each other on the Outer Circle route. The one loading passengers in Bromford Lane on the extreme left is an FOF-registered Daimler COG5 of 1939 on a shortworking to Perry Barr. The 1947 Daimler CVA6 on the right negotiates the island on its clockwise journey around the 11 bus route. The sign of The Fox and Goose public house can be seen behind car 776. These Brush-built cars were fitted with EMB Burnley bogies and were the only cars in the BCT fleet to be equipped with the EMB air wheel and track brake system. They ran with powerful Dick, Kerr DK30/1L 63hp motors. Washwood Heath drivers quite often exploited the speed potential of these cars and their bow collector current collection with some spirited running. By this time car 776 had been equipped with a trolley-pole prior to being sent to Selly Oak to work the Bristol Road routes just one month later. *A. N. H. Glover*

During 1932 and 1933 the 10 route terminus was realigned to a new terminal stub in a central reservation in Washwood Heath Road opposite The Fox and Goose public house. It might well be argued that this was less accessible for intending passengers who now had to cross at least one carriageway in order to reach a waiting tramcar. This, however, was 1930s suburbia, and with low volumes of road traffic it was seen then as a modern piece of road layout. In conjunction with the reserved side track between Chetwynd Road and the new terminus, the scheme also included a traffic island where Bromford Lane and Stechford Lane met, forming part of Birmingham's Outer Ring Road and, of course, the newly introduced Outer Circle bus route. An immaculately turned-out car 794 stands at the new terminus on 5 September 1933. *Author's collection*

ALUM ROCK

The Alum Rock 8 route was opened on 1 January 1907 and was worked by the newly opened Washwood Heath depot. It started from the second barrier from the top of Martineau Street and followed the Washwood Heath route as far as the Gate, whence it climbed Alum Rock Road through the busy Saltley shopping centre as far as Highfield Road (see the map on page 44). It was extended from there to Belchers Lane terminus at the Pelham on 14 October 1925 to serve the newly built council houses in the Cotterills Lane area. This was the last major section of new street tramway to be built in the city.

The details of the operation of the Alum Rock Road route were the same as the Washwood Heath route, and it was abandoned on the same Saturday night.

Below Although the Alum Rock route went straight on at the Gate, Saltley, the 8 service always seemed to be on the less important road. After leaving the Atkinson's-owned late-19th-century Gate public house, the trams entered the shopping centre that went to the top of the hill where the original 1907 terminus at Highfield Road was reached. On 16 August 1950 passengers are boarding car 789, which will shortly negotiate the junction with Washwood Heath Road. This area, except for the pub and a few of the shops, has barely changed over the intervening years. *R. T. Wilson*

Above right The thriving shopping centre in Alum Rock Road, seen on the same day, 16 August 1950, looking down towards the Gate junction, was very close to Saltley Gas Works, which can be seen in the background. The driver of the early postwar Austin 8 car seems unsure as to whether to pass on the inside of tram 795, which has apparently just left the stop next to the car. It will leave Saltley's bustling Victorian shopping district for the grimy industrial landscape of the River Rea valley as it crosses Saltley Viaduct. *R. T. Wilson*

Below right The Rock cinema in Alum Rock Road can be seen above the surrounding shops beyond the tram in this 17 September 1950 view. It was opened on 15 January 1934, and compared to the shops, such as the Maypole Dairy Co Ltd and The Gate Fish and Chip Saloon, it seemed the height of luxury, although the opening bill, part of which was a Laurel and Hardy short, was, perhaps, not quite what the customers expected on such an auspicious occasion. The cinema closed in 1972, the Maypole Dairy Co ceased trading many years ago and the chip shop has been replaced by much more exotic Balti-type fare. Car 770 waits to pick up passengers on the 8 route. It carries an advertisement for the *Birmingham Gazette*, a newspaper that only survived the trams by three years after 215 years of publication. *J. E. Gready*

Below In Edwardian days when the streets were gas-lit, deliveries were made by horse and cart, the safety cycle was still a novelty, and little boys' mothers were practising to be over-protective, the shops in Alum Rock Road were doing a roaring trade. Alum Rock was a thriving suburban shopping centre that had developed up the hill between the Gate Inn, which is beyond the tramcar as the last building on the left, and High Street, Saltley. An unusual feature of the shops on the right, which include the Unique Tea Company at No 20, Alum Rock Road, was that they were single-storied with a two-storey house attached behind. UEC top-covered Radial-truck car 208, in virtually original condition with open-platform vestibules and open balconies, moves down the hill towards The Gate and the junction with Washwood Heath Road. The last 17 of the class, including this one, were used when the Washwood Heath Road service was introduced, some four months after the tracks to Alum Rock were opened on 1 January 1907. *Commercial postcard*

Bottom A 1925 Austin Seven Chummy is parked outside Hunt's, gentlemen's outfitters, who are having a sale of hosiery, corsets (!), cardigans and pullovers, while next door is Albert Deakin's boot and shoe repair shop. The next shop to have its sunblinds pulled down is F. H. Prosser's double-fronted chemist and druggist's shop. The tram, which is descending Alum Rock Road from Highfield Road one lunchtime, is passing the row of shops on this side of Wright Road, where the deep shadows cast by the buildings on the right are broken by the gap of Ralph Road. The tram is No 297, a Brill 21E-trucked vehicle, which, when first delivered from UEC of Preston, was an open-topped, open-vestibuled, three-bay-bodied car that offered a very basic level of comfort, even when new in 1908. The tram had been top-covered within a few years of entering service, had been vestibuled in the mid-1920s and, other than the cars fitted with the Maley track brake and bow collectors for the Lodge Road service, No 297 was one of the last of these small trams to remain in service, being withdrawn in August 1936, though it was stored for another six months before succumbing to the scrapman's hammer. *Commercial postcard*

259-10 Alum Rock Road, Birmingham.

Above The original terminus in Alum Rock Road was here at the top of the hill at Highfield Road; car 102 is seen leaving in the direction of the distant Saltley gas holders and the city centre in about 1914. It is in almost original condition with open vestibules and 'flop-over' destination boards. Although only 30 years old, the shops have about them the well-worn look of an area past its first flush of youth. Yet it is a suburb that survives today, looking very much the same as it did in that long, hot summer before all innocence was lost. *Commercial postcard*

Below Approaching the Belisha crossing just beyond College Road on its way into town on the 8 route is bow collector car 796. It is September 1950 and in only a matter of days the sound of trams rumbling along Alum Rock Road will be no more than a memory. In the distance, passing Ludlow Road, is an FOF-registered Daimler COG5 working on the 14 bus route from Kitts Green. To the right of the tram, on the corner of College Road, is the premises of the Royal London Insurance Company, which has, at street level, all the architectural fixtures of a bank, which indeed it was, originally being a branch of the National Provincial Bank. *J. S. Webb*

Above Car 762 is photographed in Alum Rock Road on 4 September 1950 with only about a month left before the route is abandoned. It is travelling towards the city and is about half a mile from the old terminus at Highfield Road. Jephcott Road, which the tram is passing, marked a transition point in the growth of the city along this route. To the left, behind the trees, are the last Victorian/early-20th-century shops, while opposite them are some of the earliest post-First World War council houses in Birmingham. They were built in Cotterills Lane and were first occupied in 1919. This area looks very much the same today except for the now far more mature trees. *R. T. Wilson*

Below A Morrison BM-type battery-electric bread van stands at the junction of Cotterills Lane and Alum Rock Road as car 803 swings round from the nearby terminus at Belchers Lane. The 1-mile extension of the route to the Pelham Arms pub was opened on 14 October 1925, and was the last piece of street tramway opened in Birmingham; the six subsequent tramway extensions were built along reserved track and were therefore designed for faster running. *R. T. Wilson*

Above Looking in the opposite direction the cluster of shops at Belchers Lane at the terminus of the 8 tram route are seen on 4 September 1950. The conductor of car 768 is about to help the little girl on to the platform of the tram, while beyond it car 773 is waiting for 768 to depart for the city before itself entering the terminal stub. The shops are typical of the small retailers that developed in the suburbs. A butcher, tobacconist and greengrocer are to the right, while beyond the small lorry is a Timothy Whites & Taylors chemist. Next door but one is Pearks Dairies Ltd, grocers and provisioners, whose shop probably gave off that wonderful smell of smoked bacon so characteristic of such shops before the advent of the supermarket. *R. T. Wilson*

Below Car 789 stands in the terminal stub on 4 June 1950 with the Pelham Arms in the background, an imposing council estate public house built in the mid-1920s by Mitchells & Butlers. Car 789 clearly shows the advantages on a warm day of eight upper saloon windows, as every row of seats has access to an opening window. The car is in its final 1948-style livery, with advertisements for Bovril and the new Dreft washing powder; many Birmingham trams by this time could be identified from the combination of advertisements they carried. This 1950 view recalls the lack of vehicular traffic at the time - there is no other vehicle in sight! *T. J. Edgington*

PERRY BARR

This route was opened from Martineau Street to Newtown Row on 1 January 1907, and was extended to Chain Walk, just beyond Six Ways, Aston, on 23 April 1907. Unfortunately, because of problems with interworking, the through service to Perry Barr was not opened until 8 December 1909.

Starting from the top stand in Martineau Street, the 6 route followed the Washwood Heath cars along Corporation Street but carried on past the Victoria Law Courts to Corporation Place. Here it crossed through the complicated traffic island arrangement and turned into Lancaster Street, which was lined with warehouses and factories. On reaching Princip Street, the route climbed over the steep rise of the Birmingham & Fazeley Canal bridge, whose crest was marked by an ornate wrought-iron urinal.

Beyond here lay Newtown Row, with its linear shopping centre that extended as far as the Bartons Arms. On either side lay a tightly packed area of mid-19th-century housing. Immediately behind Newtown Row and parallel to it on the western side was Summer Lane. This road, through apocryphal and true stories about it, perhaps epitomised the real hard-working, hard-playing Brummie of the first half of this century.

On leaving the shops, public houses and music hall in Newtown Row, the 6 service climbed up to High Street through another shopping centre to reach Six Ways, Aston. Here the 3 route turned right into Witton Road, while the Perry Barr route continued past Chain Walk, where, for 18 months, a tram was parked every day to act as a waiting room for passengers travelling between the Chain Walk shuttle and the main service from Birmingham.

Birchfield Road gradually opened out into a tree-lined road with large Victorian villas in their own capacious grounds. The route crossed Aston Lane at the Birchfield Road shopping centre. Here was Perry Barr depot, which had been taken over from Handsworth UDC and was intermittently a running depot for the Perry Barr service. The tram route terminated just short of Perry Barr station almost outside the New Crown & Cushion public house.

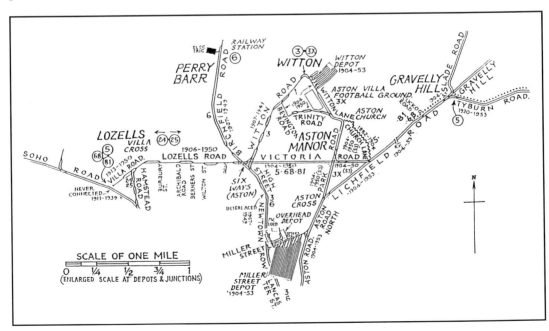

Perry Barr, Witton and Lozells routes

The 6 route was, for most of their careers, the preserve of the trams of the 1-20 class, although the two ex-CBT bogie cars, 451 and 452, were latterly to be found on it. Other newer totally enclosed trams were found on the route in later years, before the route was abandoned on 31 December 1949.

Above The 6 route to Perry Barr started at a kerbside loading barrier at the top of Martineau Street outside Preedy's tobacconist shop. In this 1949 view the passengers are boarding car 13, one of only six of the 1-20 class to survive the Second World War. They were originally built by the Electric Railway & Tramway Carriage Works Ltd (ER&TCW) in 1904 as 56-seater open-top reversed-staircase double-deckers, but cars 11-20 were quickly rebuilt with top covers by UEC, which gave them an overall height of 16ft 3in. As this was some 9 inches higher than later top-covered cars, these Miller Street-allocated trams were used almost exclusively on the 6 route, which had no height restrictions on it. The tram, once loaded, will swing into Corporation Street in front of the Cobden Hotel. The Dolcis shoe shop, in the years just after the war, had one of the potentially dangerous self-X-ray machines for viewing your own feet! *R. T. Wilson*

Above right The rather splendid late-1920s Austin crosses the tramlines from Martineau Street just after car 15 has turned down Corporation Street on the 6 route. The tram will cross Bull Street before reaching the white concrete expanse of the distant Lewis's store on the left. This was as near to the heart of Birmingham as trams ever reached. With no cross-city workings, the tram routes often had their own specific car types peculiar to that route; if the Lodge Road had the Brill-Maleys, then the 6 route had the open-balconied bogie cars. Sometimes known as the 'Old Bogies', they gave splendid service to the city. This view, taken in about 1932, shows car 15 with the gold lining-out on the dash panel that was so characteristic of the prewar livery. This car was bomb-damaged in January 1941, then stored until broken up in 1946. *R. T. Wilson*

Above Corporation Place later became a three-level road junction, but when car 10 crossed it on 18 March 1939 the two main features were, on the extreme right, the Central Fire Station, opened in 1935, and Halfords Cycle Co Ltd, behind the tram. The latter building was destroyed by fire on 12 March 1955, much to the embarrassment of the fire service. Car 10 was top-covered by G. C. Milnes, Voss & Co Ltd in March 1905, and subsequently fitted with upholstered transverse seats, EMB Burnley bogies and 40hp motors. This conversion work increased the weight by some 2½ tons, which meant that the cars' performance was not particularly sparkling. Car 10 was one of 24 trams destroyed on the night of 9-10 April 1941 when Miller Street was hit during an air raid by an oil bomb. *A. N. H. Glover*

Below Cars returning to the city via Corporation Place turned across the front of the Central Fire Station into Stafford Street, whose one-way single line took the inbound trams to Dale End. At the outer end factories like Harris & Sheldon Ltd dominated the scene. Car 570 was one of 75 UEC-bodied 62-seater trams mounted on M&G Burnley maximum traction bogies. It had been transferred to Miller Street depot after the Stratford Road abandonments of January 1937 and remained there until the BCT system closed in 1953. *R. T. Wilson*

Above At the far end of Stafford Street the splendid industrial buildings gave way to a series of rather time-worn three-storey terraces, most of which had been converted into small individual shops. The Corner Cafe seen here on the right, with its pseudo-Greek portico, looked out over the junction with Coleshill Street to the right, and to John Watt Street to the left, which was used by the Washwood Heath routes. By the mid-1950s the cafe had become the Shah Jahan, one of the first Indian restaurants in Birmingham. Car 686, built by Brush in December 1924, trundles towards this junction before running up to Dale End and the Martineau Street terminus. *F. Lloyd Jones*

Below Car 656, on the 6 route, and 811, numerically the last of the EMB air brake cars, on the 10 route, stand in Dale End on 27 December 1949. Dale End was one of the oldest streets in Birmingham, although precious little of it remains today. It was originally the main road to Lichfield and, as such in the 18th and 19th centuries, became a street of commerce and industry. John Taylor set up his japanning works, which employed over 500 people, in Crooked Lane off Dale End. In 1765 Taylor and Sampson Lloyd II set up Taylor and Lloyd's bank, which was later to become Lloyds Bank, one of the 'big four' national banks. *T. J. Edgington*

Above Travelling into the city centre along Lancaster Street, car 3 is about to cross Corporation Place and enter the one-way system that will take it to its Martineau Street terminus. On the far side of Corporation Place, guarding the entrance to the distant Stafford Street, is Joseph Gilman's drysalters on the right and Harris & Sheldon shopfitters premises. ER&TCW bogie car No 3, fitted with a Milnes, Voss top cover in March 1905 when it was just 14 months old, was numerically the earliest of the six 1-20 class that survived the war. Parked outside Halford's cycle factory to the left of the tram is a London-registered 1947 Vauxhall Twelve-Four. To the left is Corporation Street, where the tram services to Erdington ran alongside the Central Fire Station. *W. A. Camwell*

Below Looking again at the outward-going 6 service, the trams turned from Corporation Place into Lancaster Street, which would take the tram route to Newtown Row. The warehouses and factories in this wide, cobbled thoroughfare, such as Stanley Croft and Brown, Hopwood & Gilbert, tower over car 452 as it passes Lench Street. Cars 451 and 452 were, at 34ft 8in, the two longest cars in the Birmingham fleet, these stately trams being known locally as 'The Titanics'. They were fitted with Dick, Kerr DK13A 40hp motors and travelled sedately about their business until the last day of 1949, when the Perry Barr route was abandoned. Built as car 180 for CBT, 452 was originally an open-topper and subsequently, during the First World War, a single-decker used in trailer experiments on the Washwood Heath route. *D. Griffiths*

Above The other ex-CBT bogie car 'twin' was 451, which had been 178 in the original owner's fleet and which is seen here negotiating the steep Birmingham & Fazeley Canal bridge. The motorcyclist overtaking on the blind humpback bridge must have worked out the odds against another tramcar rearing up in front of him. It is December 1949 and car 451 is nearing the end of 46 years of service during which it ran some 650,000 miles. It was fitted with a CBT-built, 68-seater, five-bay body, which further emphasised the length of the tram. Car 451 is quite near the premises of William Shillock, boot and shoe manufacturer, of No 73 Newtown Row, from whose shop window on Thursday 12 September 1895 the original FA Cup was stolen. It had been on display after Aston Villa won it, beating West Bromwich Albion 1-0. *R. T. Wilson*

Above right Today this is the junction between the A34 Newtown Row dual-carriageway and the New John Street West section of the A4540 Middleway Ring Road. In the years immediately after the Second World War, Newtown Row had seen better days with many of the awful back-to-back houses still being found in its side streets, including those in nearby New Summer Street, Lower Tower Street, Hatchett Street, New John Street West and Miller Street.

Although Newtown Row was once the centre for the new town area of Aston, first mentioned in the 1780s, it was intensely developed in the 1830s and 1840s with some of the highest population densities ever achieved in the Birmingham area. On a gloomy-looking day, with Wilson's furniture store on the left, tram 583, originally one of the six trams used on the unsuccessful Hagley Road 'First Class' service of 1914, stands just beyond the New John Street West junction. The tram is almost opposite the tracks to its right that enabled trams to turn into Miller Street for depot journeys. *R. T. Wilson*

Above Car 3 stands in Newtown Row with a lazy destination number box, which had probably been turned by children riding on the balcony. It is working the 6 route and has reached St Stephen's Church, built in the Early English style in brick and sandstone and consecrated in 1844. It finally closed its doors in 1950, just a few months after the final abandonment of the Perry Barr trams. Car 3, by this time something of a venerable vehicle, seems to have a lower saloon that is at odds with the much more perpendicular upper saloon. Newtown Row continued towards the Aston Hippodrome, which is just discernible beyond the 1-20 class tram in the far distance. *F. Lloyd Jones*

Below The half-price footwear for sale at N. B. Shoes, on the corner of Inkerman Street and High Street, Newtown,

Aston, appears to be creating some interest as groups of people do their shopping one Saturday morning in November 1949. Car 581 has just turned on to the short section of interlaced track in front of 'The House That Jack Built' store, which was just beyond the shoppers to the right. The tram is just above the culverted Hockley Brook, a tributary of the River Rea, which in medieval times had been a problem to cross. Tram 581 entered service in February 1914 and was another of those used on the short-lived 'First Class' experiment along the recently opened Hagley Road route. Its dashes were painted yellow, the lower saloon seats were covered in blue plush cushions, and rubber matting was laid on the floor. Brown curtains were fitted and notices proclaiming 'First Class Car' and 'Double Fares' were displayed. *F. Lloyd Jones*

Above The 'jewel' of Newtown was undoubtedly the Barton's Arms public house, standing in the angle between High Street, to the left, and Potters Lane. The pub was built in 1901 and was designed by the James and Lister Lea company of renowned public house architects in a mock-Jacobean style for Mitchells & Butlers, which must have been something of a 'smack in the teeth' for the local Ansell's Brewery, its nearby arch-rival. With its terracotta brickwork, Minton tiling and snob screens, the Barton's Arms replaced a much earlier tavern on this site. Tram 19, still with 'flop-over' destination boards and later destined to be destroyed during the bombing of Witton depot in December 1940, stands between the Barton's Arms and the Globe Electric cinema at the bottom of High Street in about 1914. On the right is Newtown's third centre of culture. This was the Aston Hippodrome, which had been opened in 1908 with an auditorium capacity of 2,000. During this week, top of the bill is Edna Latonne, but second billing is Will Hay (1888-1949), who would achieve greater stardom in his late-1930s films. *Commercial postcard*

Right Passengers board car 677 in High Street, Newtown, in 1949. This was one of 40 trams ordered in 1924 from the Brush Electrical Company of Loughborough, who supplied the 63-seater bodies. It was mounted on EMB maximum traction bogies and fitted with English Electric 40hp motors; 33ft 6in long and weighing some 16 tons, it spent all its 29-year service life working from Miller Street depot. It stands opposite the Barton's Arms, and just visible behind the tram is the Globe Cinema (formerly the Globe Electric Palace) which was opened in August 1913 and closed in September 1955; the entrance, on the corner of New Street and High Street, was surmounted by a dome or globe-like structure. Car 677 will ascend High Street while car 570, a tram some ten years older, makes its way towards the city. *F. Lloyd Jones*

Above Car 657, one of the 1923 MRCW 637-661 class, is seen travelling towards the city on the cobbled High Street hill. The tall gabled building is the impressive Barton's Arms public house; opened in 1901, this Grade II listed building, one of the most famous pubs in Birmingham, is noted for its tile painted walls, stained glass windows and wooden snob screens in the smoke rooms. *R. T. Wilson*

Below The distant clock stands on the Midland Bank's premises at the corner of Lozells Road and Birchfield Road at Six Ways, Aston, and marks one of the most complicated sections of trackwork in Birmingham, with five of the six roads carrying tramlines. The 5 route, Birmingham's only inter-urban service, from Lozells to Gravelly Hill, crossed High Street, Six Ways, Aston, where car 583 is standing, and went into Victoria Road, which is on the distant right behind the Morris 10 saloon. The steep hill of Witton Road took the 3 route towards Witton depot and Villa Park, a service withdrawn in early September 1939. Only Alma Street, which carried the 33 Kingstanding bus route and ran behind the buildings on the left, did not carry a tram route. In this 1949 view, the tram is passing Morrison Electricar DV 4-type battery electric dustcart No 221 (FVP 85), built in 1940 and enjoying a working career of nearly 25 years. Birmingham had the largest fleet of battery electric dustcarts in the country, and between 1918 and 1971 operated 262 vehicles. *R. T. Wilson*

Above 'Aston bogie' car 17 is about to rattle over the Lozells tram tracks at Six Ways, Aston, in the shadow of the extravagantly Dutch-gabled National Provincial Bank. The tramcar is working towards Perry Barr on the 6 service during 1949. Sandwiched between the 1938 Jowett car, standing underneath the Nestlés Milk sign in Victoria Road and the almost new Hillman Minx Phase III, is bus No 1542 (GOE 542), a Metro-Cammell-bodied Daimler CVA6, which has come up the steep hill in Witton Road on the 7 bus route to Portland Road. A similar bus, No 1485 (GOE 485) is travelling in the opposite direction on this cross-city working and is going to Perry Common. Following the tram is a prewar Morris-Commercial 30cwt C-type, while the larger lorry is a CVF 'Equi-load' model from the same manufacturer. Towering above them and all the shops in High Street is the eastern-styled Orient

Cinema, opened on 4 August 1930 and closed in February 1964 with a film ironically titled *Thing That Couldn't Die*. *G. F. Douglas/A. D. Packer*

Below On leaving Six Ways the Perry Barr route reached Chain Walk. For nearly two years, from 1907, this was the terminus – through working to Perry Barr was prohibited because of a dispute with Handsworth UDC. Passengers had to change from one Corporation car to another; as a result of this difficulty, it was the practice to take a spare tram from Birchfield Road depot each morning and park it at Chain Walk to serve as a waiting room for transferring passengers. Here car 579 leaves the short section of single-line track at Mansfield Road on its inward-bound journey. *F. Lloyd Jones*

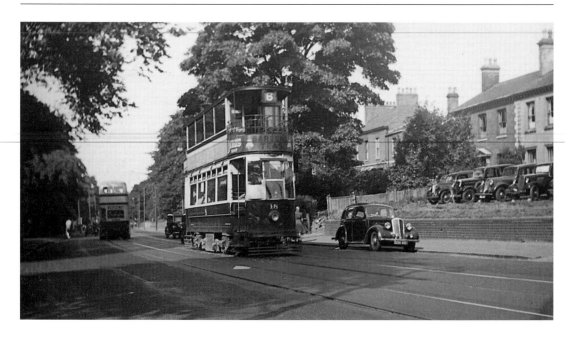

Above One of the great delights in looking at old photographs of street scenes is identifying the long-forgotten models built by long-forgotten car manufacturers. Overtaking the parked Standard Flying Light Twelve is tramcar 18, travelling away from Perry Barr along Birchfield Road on the 6 route, and one of only six of the 1-20 class to survive wartime bombing. It is going towards the splendid 'high' Victorian Holy Trinity Church of 1864, which still stands today at the nearby junction with Trinity Road, but partly hidden by the Birchfield Road flyover. The houses lining this section of Birchfield Road, which until 1912 were in Handsworth UDC, were among the best-quality residential properties in the area. Unfortunately, the ones to the right of the tram would suffer planning blight for many years, which is why a particular front garden is being used as a second-hand car lot. Awaiting sale is a Ford Y Type, an Austin Light 12/4, a Hillman and a unidentified small van. *J. S. Webb*

Below Picking up passengers at the tram stop in Birchfield Road between Thornbury Road and The Broadway is car 8, which by this date, 1949, would have been about 46 years old; it was withdrawn in October of that year due to accident damage, some two months before the final five survivors of the rest of these original BCT 'Aston' bogies. The row of shops on the right dates from the 1920s, as does the Perry Barr branch of the Municipal Bank on the corner of The Broadway. In the distance is the Birchfield cinema, which dated from 25 September 1913 when it was also known as the Picturedrome. From August 1930, this cinema was always the poor relation to the lavish Art Deco-styled Odeon, further up Birchfield Road, which was the very first Odeon cinema in the country built by the Oscar Deutsch chain. *Author's collection*

Above The Perry Barr shopping centre developed on either side of the Aston Lane junction. There was a small row of early-20th-century shops in Birchfield Road dominated by the Birchfield cinema, which is being passed by car 345 working the 6 route in this rare 1946 view. The tram is still painted in the wartime grey livery that it retained until withdrawal in August 1947. Car 20, in front of it, has the prewar livery with cream-painted rocker panels. To the left is Birchfield Road garage, which had been taken over from Handsworth UDC in 1911. The two BCT buses in the distance are a Daimler COG5, still with khaki-painted roof and rear dome, and MOS Brush-rebodied AEC 'Regent' No 397 (OG 397), of 1930 vintage. A BMMO FEDD, one of only three to be built as a full-front vehicle, can also be seen, still in its prewar livery. *V. E. Burrows*

Below On a gloomy Wednesday 28 December 1949 car 18 stands at the New Crown & Cushion terminus near Perry Barr railway station, posters in its window announcing the imminent abandonment of the tram service just three days later. Perry Barr was the city boundary until 1928 and by that date the days of tramway extensions were over. In fact, the 33 bus route to Kingstanding was opened in 1929 and this effectively ended any chance of extending the 6 route. The terminus, served faithfully by the 1-20 class, therefore remained at Perry Barr for some 40 years. Note the Foden BRS lorry crossing the railway bridge. *A. N. H. Glover*

WITTON

The 3 route left Six Ways, Aston, and descended the steep hill in Witton Road past the former Aston Council House and through sections of double and single line before arriving at Witton Square where it met the 3X route (see the map on page 68). The 3 route had been opened by CBT in 1904 and was taken over on 1 January 1912. It was the only branch off the main 6 route and was part of a circular service with the 3X route around Witton; however, the 3 route was suspended for the duration of the Second World War after 9 September 1939, and was not restored at the end of the hostilities, although the line remained intact until 1947.

The 3X route followed the Aston Road routes as far as Aston Cross, where it climbed up Park Road between Ansell's Brewery and the nearby HP Sauce factory in Tower Street. It crossed the junction with Victoria Road before passing Aston Hall on a 1 in 20 descent to turn left in front of the splendid Aston parish church. This hill caused two car-wrecking accidents, with No 323 in 1932 and 714 in 1940 succumbing to brake failure and driver error.

The 3X route then passed Villa Park, opposite a line of very distinctive pre-First World War semi-detached houses across the road from the ground, before reaching the terminus at the Witton Arms public house opposite the former CBT depot. The car would then continue back to the city via Witton Road and Six Ways, Aston.

Always in BCT days associated with the 301 class, the 3X route, which had survived in a truncated form, lasted until it was replaced by the 39 bus, the last trams running on 31 December 1949. The depot remained in use until 1953, and as a result the line remained intact until the closure of the system.

On a quiet Sunday 12 March 1933, UEC-built four-wheel, open-balcony car 309 approaches the junction with Bull Street. The still gleaming white Portland Stone frontage of the three-year-old Lewis's department store is just visible on the left, while the building with the 'lighthouse' above the same junction is occupied at ground level by Dunn's the hatter and gentlemen's outfitter, which had competition on the nearer corner from Montague Burton, whose '30 Shilling Tailors' shop front is immediately to the right of the tram. Car 308 has just left Martineau Street and is on its way to Witton via Aston Cross on the 3X route. Just under three months later, only the tram would be able to travel in the direction seen here as the infamous city centre one-way scheme would be implemented and the little Austin Seven would have to turn round. *S. L. Smith*

Above The 3X route was the anti-clockwise section of the service to Witton until the outbreak of war, when its other half, the 3 route, was closed on 11 September 1939. The 3X followed the Erdington group of tram routes along Aston Road as far as Aston Cross, where the 3X forked to the left of the large Ansell's Brewery and climbed Park Road. At 1.30pm Brush-built tram 610 has just descended Park Road and is standing by the famous public clock before moving off towards the city centre. No 610 would only just survive the closure of the Witton route on 31 December 1949 as it was involved in a severe accident in February 1950 and subsequently withdrawn. *G. F. Douglas*

Below The main Lichfield Road routes can be seen in the distance, with a tram on the 79 service standing at Aston Cross in front of Ansell's Brewery. Alongside the brewery ran Park Road, the scene of this photograph; the majority of this link between Aston Cross and Witton was swept away when the Aston Expressway was opened in May 1972. As well as being part of the 3X tram route to Witton depot, Park Road was also used for football specials to Villa Park, such as that being operated by car 691. It has just passed a horse and cart, appropriately carrying wooden beer barrels, and is climbing past the rather shabby shops opposite the brewery. It is late 1949 and Hollings Cafe, with a few pieces of decorative tinsel in the window, is offering the bargain of five mince pies for a shilling. *R. T. Wilson*

Above Once at the top of Park Road the 3X route crossed the inter-urban 5 service at Victoria Road and descended the steep hill towards Aston parish church, with its graceful 15th-century tower. Park Road itself was a strange contrast. Beyond the Wolverhampton-registered Hillman Minx lies Aston Hall and its surrounding park; built by the Holte family between 1618 and 1635, it is one of the finest Jacobean houses in the country. Yet on this grey Wednesday, 28 December 1949, car 631 climbs past the Sycamore public house and the Victorian terraces that look even more uninviting than normal. *A. N. H. Glover*

Below Car 537, one of the former open-balconied UEC bogie cars, is seen at Aston parish church in 1949. This tram had previously been at Rosebery Street depot, but after the closure of the Ladywood route it was transferred to Witton depot, where it stayed until early 1950. It is standing approximately where car 714 overturned in March 1940, injuring some 30 passengers. This wartime accident was caused when the tram failed to make the turn into Witton Lane at Park Road when the driver lost control; the roof and the upper deck broke apart. In the resultant enquiry the driver was blamed for failing to make the compulsory stop on Park Lane hill. *R. T. Wilson*

Top A young boy and his mother, walking alongside the grounds of Aston Hall, look at the trams standing in Trinity Road awaiting the football fans from Villa Park on 15 February 1938. Leading the line is open-balcony four-wheel tramcar 349, and immediately behind are two of Washwood Heath depot's 762 class bow collector trams, which were only ever used away from their native haunts on Villa Park football specials. On this particular occasion, in the middle of the season after they had returned as champions to the First Division, it would be the Aston Villa supporters who would be rejoicing from the crowd of 27,500 as the home team comprehensively beat Huddersfield Town 4-0. *R. T. Wilson*

Middle Witton Square, at the end of Witton Lane, marked the terminus of the 3X route. As already mentioned, until the outbreak of the Second World War it had been a circular route; the 3 service, which came down Witton Road from Six Ways, Aston, also terminated here, and its track can be seen turning to the left in front of the butcher's shop beyond the waiting tram. These lines were subsequently only used for football specials. Car 610, one of the 1920 cars with Brush bodies, open balconies and Brush Burnley maximum traction bogies, stands at the Aston Hotel on 17 July 1949, between the entrance tracks to Witton depot and next to the Bundy Clock. This car suffered severe accident damage in February 1950 and was broken up the following month. *C. C. Thornburn*

Bottom Witton depot was originally opened in 1882 by the Birmingham & Aston Tramways for its steam trams. Eventually it was taken over by BCT on 1 January 1912 and was in regular use until 30 September 1950, when it was relegated to a store for withdrawn trams. On 23 June 1950 four tramcars stand at each of the entrance gates, when the 3X service had just over five months to run. The nearest tram is car 609, a

Brush-bodied 62-seater built in 1920 with open balconies, mounted on Brush Burnley bogies and by this time powered by 63hp DK 30/1 motors; it survived in service until just before the final abandonments of July 1953. The three remaining trams, Nos 342, 372 and 367, are UEC-bodied 52-seaters mounted on 7ft 6in flexible-axle swing-yoke trucks powered by 40hp Dick, Kerr DK 13A motors.

No 342 was the first tram in the fleet to be equipped with enclosed balconies, in January 1921. Although satisfactory from a protection aspect, the conversion was aesthetically ungainly, earning the tram the somewhat unsympathetic nickname 'The Armoured Car'. It was the second design, built on car 347 (see page 102), that became the Birmingham standard. *L. W. Perkins*

Below Witton Square, with its small shopping centre sandwiched between Witton station and Aston Lane, was just a few yards beyond Witton depot. On 21 September 1938 car 213 stands on the curve into Witton Road when working on the 3X route. When new in early 1907 this tram was mounted on an M&G 8ft 6in Radial truck, but these were quickly found to be unsatisfactory due to their lack of return action when coming off curves, resulting in

car 213 being the subject of early experiments by being fitted with a UEC swing-link 7ft 6in truck of the type that was to be adopted on the 301 class trams. Car 213 retained this truck until it was withdrawn from Witton depot, redundant following the 2 April 1939 closure of the 'mainline' West Bromwich and Dudley services. The 301 class four-wheelers were retained because of their lower height, but all the 71 class trams were withdrawn. *W. A. Camwell*

Below Standing in Bevington Road at the end of a row of eight Villa Park Football Special trams in 1949 is car 777, parked in this side street during a match at Villa Park. This tram, in common with all the 762 class cars from Washwood Heath depot, was fitted with a Fischer bow collector. Until that depot's closure to trams in October 1950, the Villa Park excursions were virtually these trams' only sojourn away from the 8 and 10 routes. Car 777 later became the tram that closed the Bristol Road routes at about midnight on 5 July 1952. Darlington's ironmongery, with its galvanised buckets, pans and sundry items of domestic drudgery, is obviously finding the competition with the match at Villa Park a little too much – trade seems a little slow in Bevington Road on this November day. *R. T. Wilson*

Above UEC car 346 descends Witton Road just before the Great War on what would later become the 3 route. It has arrived at this point having left Martineau Street and gone by way of Corporation Place, Lancaster Street, Newtown Row and Six Ways, Aston. This Witton-allocated tram has just negotiated the loop on the curve in Witton Road at the Albert Road junction outside the former Aston Manor Town Hall. This building enjoyed a brief period as the Borough Council headquarters between 1903 to 1911; by this time the building had become a library. The tram has a 'flop-over' destination board on the upper saloon balcony; these were removed in 1915 and the letter 'W' hidden in the dark recesses of the canopy. *Author's collection*

Right Standing in High Street, Aston, near the Barton's Arms is car 328, which is being employed on the 3 route. It has just passed New Street and has stopped outside Mellow & Son, grocers and provision merchants. The tram will climb up the quite steep hill to Six Ways, Aston, before turning right into Witton Road. On this rainy Saturday, 1 April 1939, the day that the Spanish Civil War ended, car 328's driver has lowered his canvas rain shield, while the leading saloon doors, with their etched Birmingham Municipal Bank key symbol, are firmly shut against the elements. No 328 would soldier on throughout the Second World War and serve for another ten and a half years before being finally broken up at Moseley Road depot. *L. W. Perkins*

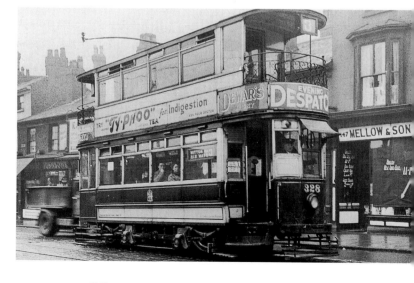

LOZELLS

The Lozells route was Birmingham's only real inter-suburban tram service. Opened between Lozells and Gravelly Hill by CBT on 7 May 1906, it was taken over by BCT on 1 January 1912 and abandoned on 30 September 1950. It was always operated by Witton depot and in BCT days used 301 class four-wheelers and 512 class bogie cars.

The route terminated at Villa Cross but was extended by BCT to Villa Road on 8 January 1913, within a few yards of the main Soho Road trams, although there was never any physical connection.

On leaving the terminus, the 5 route went past some of the large Victorian villas that typified residential Handsworth, before arriving at the Hamstead Road junction where the 24 and 25 routes turned into Villa Road. The shopping centre here was known as 'the village' and was for many years one of the better-known suburban shopping centres in Birmingham.

After passing Villa Cross, the cinema with the large ornate rose window above the entrance,

and the Villa Cross public house in the angle between Lozells Road and Heathfield Road, the trams used sections of double and single track through the mixed Victorian residential and shopping area to Six Ways, Aston, which, as has already been mentioned, was one of the most complicated track layouts on the BCT system. Crossing the junction, the route then went along Victoria Road and intersected the 3X route at Park Road. As Victoria Road descended to join Lichfield Road, so the size and quality of the houses deteriorated.

The route turned left into Lichfield Road and followed the Aston Road routes to Gravelly Hill. Here at the tram terminus the cars unloaded at the shelters before turning into Tyburn Road and reversing on the central reservation before returning to the shelters to load up. At peak times the route was extended along Tyburn Road to Fort Dunlop as a 63 route. It was also extended to Erdington as a 68 tram on Sundays until 1923, and to Pype Hayes as an 81 on summer Sundays from 1928 to 1930.

The western terminus of the Lozells route was in Villa Road, but although it was just a few yards away from the tracks in Soho Road that carried the routes to Handsworth and West Bromwich, a connecting line was never built. It is 7.35am on Tuesday 12 July 1949, and four-wheeled UEC open-balcony car 339 has had the 68, Erdington route, wound on to the blind especially for the photographer – this route was a Sunday working and

was abandoned in 1923. Behind is Brush totally enclosed bogie car 611. There is a family resemblance between the two trams, but perhaps it is surprising to realise that the larger of the cars is, in fact, only nine years newer. Car 339 was withdrawn and broken up in October 1949, while 611 was taken out of service at the abandonment of the Lozells route on 30 September 1950. *W. A. Camwell*

The busy junction of Villa Road and Hamstead Road at Lozells marked the start of the Villa Cross shopping centre. Known as 'the village', as if to emphasise that nature Bywater's shop on the left, which sold the most wonderful steak and kidney pies covered by delicious crusty pastry, was embellished with mock-Elizabethan timber decoration. Brush-bodied, totally enclosed car 589, mounted on Brush-manufactured Burnley-type maximum traction bogies, is working on the 5 route towards the Villa Cross public house. It waits as UEC-built open-balcony four-

wheeler car 387 works up towards the Villa Road terminus. Following this tram is bus 814 (BOP 814), bound for Hockley garage; a 1936 Daimler COG5, its original body was destroyed by bomb damage, and it received an English Electric body in January 1942 that had been designed for Manchester Corporation. On the gable end is an advertisement for Phillips' Grand Cut pipe tobacco, which was a brand promoted as being mild, but wasn't! *G. F. Douglas*

Above For many years sisters Julia and Agnes Bendall owned the extravagantly styled shop on the corner of Villa Road and Hamstead Road. The ladies were bakers who had another three outlets in the area as well as their most prestigious premises in Broad Street. Next door, in Villa Road, is Perth Dye Works. On this sunny, early afternoon view in the early 1920s, nearly all the shops beyond the tram have their canvas sunblinds pulled down over the pavements. This late-Victorian row of 12 shops represented perhaps the most impressive buildings in Villa Road. Beyond the tram, on the corner of Lozells Road and Heathfield Road, is the original Villa Cross Hotel; this 18th-century building had variously been used as a school and a music hall, and would be replaced by the end of the decade. The tracks in the foreground turning into Hamstead Road were used by the clockwise 24 and anti-clockwise 25 routes, which had been introduced within

weeks of each other just before the First World War. The Hamstead Road tracks and the 25 route were abandoned on 7 August 1933, leaving Hamstead Road 'tramless'. The tramcar is 381, a 50-seat four-wheeler built by UEC and delivered in November 1912. It is working on the 5 route to Gravelly Hill and would survive until October 1950. *Commercial postcard*

Below The police sergeant ambles past the few browsing shoppers in Villa Road as car 562, unusually carrying advertisements for two different brands of salad cream, works its way through the single-line section on the 63 route on its way from Fort Dunlop. Beyond distant 1947 Daimler CVG6 bus No 1580 (GOE 580) is the Villa Cross public house. This Ansell's pub had replaced an 18th-century inn during the 1920s and continued to serve this residential area until its closure in the mid-1980s. *R. T. Wilson*

Top Almost opposite the Villa Cross public house and the site of an old steam tram coal depot near the junction with Hunters Road, was a row of mid-Victorian shops, which included the Little Gem boot repairers, owned by a Mr Ballard, while behind the tram stop is the Court Steam Laundry. The purposefully striding woman is walking past the double-fronted shop of Price & Oliver, builders' merchants. Just visible above open-balconied four-wheel tram 372 is the Aston Villa Methodist Church on the corner of George Street; its principal claim to fame was that some of the young men who worshipped there were also members of the Wesleyan cricket team, and under a gas light in nearby Heathfield Road in 1874 they formed Aston Villa FC. Standing behind car 372 on 12 July 1950 is another four-wheeler, 320, and car 562, a totally enclosed bogie car. *Author's collection*

Middle Beyond Six Ways lay Victoria Road, and on a dim afternoon in late 1949 car 705 attracts the attention of a little girl as it clatters past. It was a notoriously noisy tram, having retained its spur gearing, while its 16 tons are no doubt taking their toll on what looks like fairly poor-quality track. In February 1926, when only a few months old, this car had been experimentally fitted with a pair of GEC 70hp motors; the contrast with its normal GEC WT 32H 40hp motors must have been impressive. As a result, Brush cars 512-536 were re-equipped with what proved to be the highest-horsepower motors fitted to trams in Birmingham. Car 705 is passing Wilton Street, and Abbott's furniture store dominates one side of the junction; its advertisements seem to be promoting the company and its merits rather than the furniture. This is not really surprising, as much of the furniture sold at that time was of a limited range due to the early postwar restrictions. *R. T. Wilson*

Bottom On a rainy day in September 1950 a couple of men run for the loading tram at the junction of Lozells Road and Six Ways, Aston. On the left is the imposing Portland-stone frontage of the Midland Bank, which although single-storey seems to give the junction a gravitas only matched by the towered premises of the National Provincial Bank, beyond the Bradford van parked next to the tram stop on the right. Above the tram, on the corner of Victoria Road and Witton Road, is the tower of Christ Church Baptist Chapel, founded in 1866 and, after many years of dereliction, converted into luxury flats in the 1990s. *R. T. Wilson*

Below Six Ways, Aston, was a busy junction even in the Edwardian period. CBT opened its new route between Six Ways and Aston Cross, via Park Road and Victoria Road, on 27 October 1904. On 7 May 1907 the route was extended from Lozells to Gravelly Hill after the old arched brick LNWR bridge at Aston station in Lichfield Road was replaced on 23 March 1906 by a girder bridge. CBT tram 238, built by Brush in 1904 on Lycett & Conaty 8ft

6in trucks, has arrived at Six Ways junction from Lozells Road, with Alma Street and High Street to the left and Birchfield Road to the right, and will proceed into Victoria Road. In later years this tram would become Birmingham Corporation's No 497 and be transformed by receiving a top cover and platform vestibules. *Author's collection*

Bottom The decorative spire of Christ Church Baptist Chapel is just visible in the background near Six Ways, Aston, having been passed by tramcar 621 in Victoria Road during the early summer of 1950. This 1920-built Brush-bodied eight-wheeler, working on the 5 route towards Gravelly Hill, is being followed by a 1937 Standard Flying Twelve. To the right of the tram is the Ansell's-owned White Swan Hotel on the corner of Whitehead Road. No 621 was not to survive much longer, being involved in an accident in July 1950 and broken up at Witton two months later. It is interesting that Whitehead Road, which linked High Street, at Six Ways, with Bevington Road at the rear of Aston Hall's grounds, merited three central bollards, the middle one being topped by a gas lamp. *Author's collection*

Above Victoria Road crossed the 3X route at its junction with Park Road, then went down a steady gradient to meet the Lichfield Road tram routes. Working up the hill towards Six Ways, Aston, is tram 560, a 1913 UEC-bodied bogie car, held at the traffic lights as a two-door Austin A40 Dorset pulls out of Park Road alongside the Queen's Arms public house. The houses on the left dated from the end of the 1850s, most of this area having been built up during that time. Immediately to the right of the tram is a single track that enabled trams to turn right into Park Road and gain access to Witton depot. This turn was to prove valuable on the last day of tramcar operation in the city as it was used by trams coming off service in Lichfield Road that were going to Witton for scrapping. Parked on the left, almost outside the police station, is a Fordson AA 30cwt van, while in the distance is an ERF lorry. *R. T. Wilson*

Below Looking in the opposite direction, car 342 is working the 5 route in 1950 and has reached the junction of the curve into Park Road. No 342 was originally a standard member of the 100-strong 301 class, with open balconies on a four-wheel truck. With the general improvement of tramway design welcomed by the public, BCT saw the value of enclosing the balconies on its trams. Unfortunately, the Board of Trade frowned upon double-deck narrow-gauge four-wheel tramcars being totally enclosed, and only gave 'temporary' permission for 342 and the more successful 347 to be rebuilt (see also page 83), although both ran until 1950 as totally enclosed four-wheelers. *R. T. Wilson*

Above On a sunny day in the summer of 1949, Brush-built car 618 stands at the bottom of Victoria Road on the 5 route to Gravelly Hill. The dismounted cyclist watches both the tram and the young lad beyond the tram speeding away along Lichfield Road on his racy drop-handlebar sports bike. The tram driver meanwhile looks to his right into Lichfield Road towards Aston Cross for any other traffic, and once the road is clear he will accelerate around the corner. The building on the right with the advertisement for cigarettes on the gable-end is at the corner of Victoria Road and Church Lane, while behind the tram and beyond the Belisha beacon a Fordson ice-cream delivery van speeds up the hill in Victoria Road towards the Park Road junction. *R. T. Wilson*

Below Looking towards Aston station, two trams working on the 5 route pass each other. The 19th-century terraces on the right in Lichfield Road at the Victoria Road junction were swept away in the early 1970s as part of a road-widening scheme, although, strangely, the public houses, on the same line of frontage, were retained. Car 629 is loading up with passengers before taking the tracks in the foreground into Victoria Road; it is one of 26 of the 587 class that will go to the scrapman after the closure of the Lozells route and the Alum Rock and Washwood Heath routes. The identity of the 301 class open-balcony four-wheeler tram is hidden by the Austin 8hp car. Peeking between the trams is an early postwar underfloor Midland Red bus working into Birmingham. *W. A. Camwell*

Above In order to return from Gravelly Hill to Lozells, the 5 route turned on to the reserved track in Tyburn Road and used the first crossover to reverse to the Gravelly Hill tram shelters opposite the row of shops seen in the previous photograph. Originally known as Salford Bridge Road and renamed on 25 November 1920, Tyburn Road was built with reserved track and was a joint venture between the Transport Department and the Dunlop Tyre Company, which contributed to the cost. Just visible behind the advertising hoardings on the left is the sandstone hill that had to be cut through for Tyburn Road to be linked to Gravelly Hill. Car 720 has had its pole turned prior to moving over the crossover on 29 July 1939. This car would later be badly damaged when Witton depot was hit by a bomb on the night of Wednesday 4 December 1940. It was never repaired and was broken up at Moseley Road depot in May 1946. *H. B. Priestley*

Below The 5 route was inherited from CBT on 1 January 1912, originally running between Villa Cross and Gravelly Hill, but on 8 January 1913 extended to the Villa Road-Soho Road junction, which remained its westerly terminus until the route closed. At the Tyburn Road end, the route briefly had a Bank Holiday extension, for about three years until 1923, to Erdington as the 68 route, while between 1928 and 1930 it went along Tyburn Road to serve Pype Hayes Park, as the 81 service. A branch line was opened off Tyburn Road on 13 February 1930 to the large Fort Dunlop factory, which was used by the 5 route during peak periods and at shift change-over times, as well as by the more usual 63 service. It was for this reason that, following tram replacement, the bus service was given its own route number of 40. On 24 July 1950 UEC-bodied four-wheel car 372 has just left the impressive shelters that stood in front of the Fort Dunlop factory, which survives today as a proposed penthouse-flat-cum-shopping complex. The tram has crossed the crest of the bridge over the Birmingham & Fazeley Canal, in company with a Fordson EO4C van and a 1938 Hillman Minx. *G. F. Douglas*

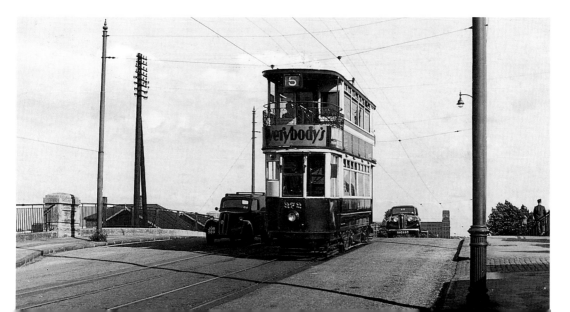

ASTON ROAD ROUTES

The first electric tram route in Birmingham owned and operated by the Corporation formed the basis of the three main routes along Aston Road, to Erdington (2), Short Heath (78), and Pype Hayes (79).

The first route opened on Monday 4 January 1904 from Steelhouse Lane, initially to the Aston Corporation boundary at Aston Brook Street, but extended about a quarter of a mile across the Aston UDC boundary to Aston Cross on 16 June 1904. The cars that inaugurated this service were of the 1-20 class, large open-top 56-seater Brill 22E bogie cars built by the Electric Railway & Tramway Carriage Works Ltd (ER&TCW). By March 1905 the first ten had been top-covered and the remainder were completed in July 1907; this precluded them from passing beneath Aston railway bridge, and for most of the remainder of their careers they plied the nearby Perry Barr route.

A second service operated by the CBT depot at Witton ran from Aston Cross to Gravelly Hill along Lichfield Road and used single-deck cars and even some converted 'toast-rack' cable cars in order to get under Aston station bridge. After the bridge was raised, in March 1906, CBT used its standard 'Aston'-type four-wheelers, some of which were subsequently taken over by BCT in 1911.

On 22 April 1907, after much discussion of through running over Aston tracks, Birmingham trams, in the form of the small open-topped 21 class cars, reached Erdington. This later became the 2 route and was the main service along the Aston and Lichfield Roads.

The stub terminus in Steelhouse Lane was near to both the main shopping thoroughfare of Bull Street and the Great Western Railway's Snow Hill station in Colmore Row. The trams descended Steelhouse Lane, passing between the Law Courts and main city police station on one side and the General Hospital on the other. They then crossed the wide expanse of Corporation Place, crossing the Perry Barr route before travelling through an area of Victorian shops and three-storey terraced housing in Aston Street, Gosta Green and Aston Road.

From the Dartmouth Street junction to Aston Cross, the main road traversed a long row of small family-type shops and factories. Between the Birmingham & Fazeley Canal and the eastern side of Aston Road North lay an area of small workshops and factories that continued to Aston Cross. This five-way junction saw the 3X tram and the Villa Park football specials continue in a northerly direction towards Aston Hall and the Witton terminus just beyond the depot, while the main route swung in front of Ansell's Brewery, leaving behind the smells of brewer's malt mixed with the vinegar from Garton's HP Sauce factory.

Lichfield Road began to descend towards Aston station after the Lozells tram service came in on the western side from Victoria Road. The route then went through an area of yet more Victorian terraced housing until it reached Aston station bridge.

Beyond the bridge was an industrial area as far as the open expanse of Salford Park. Opposite was Cuckoo Road, which led by way of a humped-back bridge to the terminus of the first electric tram route to be abandoned, the Nechells service.

The area from Aston Bridge station was a mixed residential and industrial area and really marked the limit of pre-1914 urban expansion. The junction at Salford Bridge at the bottom of Gravelly Hill was the point where the three main Aston Road routes split. The 2 route carried on up Gravelly Hill through an area of superior Edwardian housing towards Six Ways, Erdington, while the Slade Road and Short Heath route turned left towards Stockland Green, and the Pype Hayes services turned right into the reserved track in Tyburn Road.

All three routes were operated mainly by all-electric bogie cars after the mid-1920s, with the MRCW 637 class and the Brush-built 662 class being allocated for nearly all their working lives until the final abandonment on Saturday 4 July 1953.

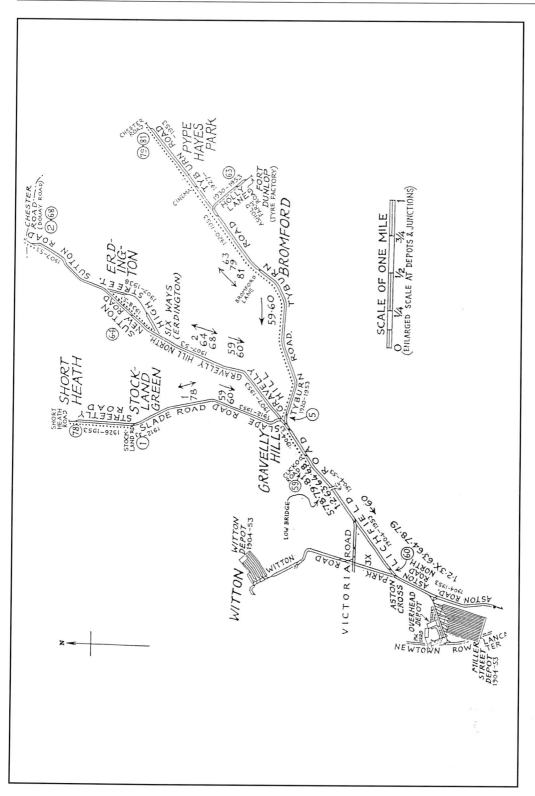

Aston Road routes

Aston Road and Lichfield Road

The three main services along Lichfield Road shared a common city terminus in Steelhouse Lane. In this 1938 view a Standard saloon turns from Bull Street into Colmore Row while in the distance a 637 class tram, resplendent in its lined-out prewar livery, stands at the terminus outside the Gaumont cinema on the 2 route; the inspector and conductor, who are standing in front of their tram, have conspired to hide its identity. This part of the city has now completely disappeared, with a pedestrian underpass and the new Wesleyan Insurance building dominating the scene today. *Author's collection*

Top Birmingham's last tramcar was No 616, which stands at the Steelhouse Lane terminus outside the Wesleyan & General building on Saturday 4 July 1953. This overhead view shows that despite the untidy end to the system, the population of Birmingham wanted to give the trams a worthy send-off. Car 616 left the city centre at 11.00am, daubed with 'Birmingham's Last Tram' along the waist panels and 'The End' on both dashes. It was a sad and rather inauspicious end to 49 years of tramcar operation in the city, and it was a great pity that a more formal official ceremony could not have taken place. No 616, carrying the Lord Mayor's party, followed similar car 623 to Erdington before returning to Miller Street for the last time. *L. W. Perkins collection*

Middle In 1950 two bogie cars, Brush-bodied No 683 of 1924 on the 79 route and 573, a UEC-bodied tram on the 2 route, are about to pass over the crossover outside the Gaumont cinema in Steelhouse Lane, whose canopy can be seen on the left. Today all this is just a memory; the trams have obviously gone, but so has everything else. This part of Steelhouse Lane is the site of a gyratory traffic system outside the *Birmingham Post & Mail* building in Colmore Circus. In this more leisurely scene, one can only wonder if the woman on the extreme right ever did pluck up enough courage to have her hair tinted. *A. B. Cross*

Bottom The delights of the Queen's Head public house do not seem to be able to entice any of the people in Steelhouse Lane as MRCW-bodied car 646 climbs the hill from the General Hospital towards the distant Gaumont cinema and the Wesleyan & General building in early 1953. The tram is carrying one of the most common advertisements to appear in later years on Birmingham trams, for '3-In-One' oil, which was used extensively on the balcony panels of bogie cars from June 1951. Yet again, the small amount of vehicular traffic is noticeable, but more modern cars are beginning to appear on the scene, such as the Vauxhall Wyvern in the middle of the road, while beyond the tram is parked a Morris Oxford and a Jaguar Mark VII. *C. C. Thornburn*

Above Two cars, Nos 700 and 694, neither carrying advertisements, travel up Steelhouse Lane from Corporation Place and past the General Hospital. Built in 1897 using terracotta brickwork, the hospital was designed by the Victorian architect William Henman, who also built the Midland Hotel in the city centre. Opposite Whittall Street, soon to become the inward unloading terminus for the tram-replacement bus services for the Aston Road routes, is the rear of the Steelhouse Lane police station and the Victoria Law Courts. Its frontage on Corporation Street is a wonderful piece of late-19th-century civic pride, combining Gothic and Renaissance styles with terracotta brickwork. *F. Lloyd Jones*

Below The last service tram to leave the Steelhouse Lane terminus was Brush-bodied 63-seater No 690, fitted with English Electric DK 30B 40hp motors. It was working to Erdington on the 2 route, and the next intending passengers would have to board No 2301 (JOJ 301), an exposed-radiator Crossley DD42/6, which would be the first replacement 64 bus. Car 690 is passing the General Hospital at the bottom of Steelhouse Lane and will swing to its right in order to enter Corporation Place. The abandonment of the trams caused quite a outflowing of grief for the passing of an era, and many people lined the route or, as here, leaned out of the hospital windows, in order to pay their last respects. This tram, however, had a partial afterlife as its motors, gears, wheels, axles and axleboxes were sold for further use on the Llandudno & Colwyn Bay Electric Railway. *R. Knibbs*

Above At exactly 5.30pm on 6 June 1953, just one month before the final abandonment, car 541, on the left, leaves the city on the 79 route, while car 696 is coming into the city from Short Heath. The trams are passing through the traffic island in Central Place; the Aston Road routes went straight on in the direction from which the rebuilt Midland Red Daimler CWA6 is coming. The replacing bus services would use Corporation Street to the left by the Central Fire Station's main entrance; this imposing building was opened by HRH the Duke of Kent on 2 December 1935, and replaced a large area of early Victorian shops and housing. Just visible on the Fire Station is the bunting from the Coronation celebrations that had taken place just four days earlier. On that Saturday there had been a Coronation procession, involving some 7,000 troops, and this had caused the temporary closure of most of the city centre roads. *L. W. Perkins*

Below Looking in the opposite direction, we see two MRCW trams, Nos 651 and 657, travelling down a nearly deserted Aston Street towards Central Place, with the Central Fire Station to their right. These cars, despite all the problems incurred with their delivery dates in 1923, put in excellent service, covering a maximum mileage of 941,000 in 30 years. Their 40hp motors did not exactly give sparkling performance, but as they operated their entire lives from Miller Street depot, the extra power required on the hillier routes, such as Bristol Road, was not necessary. The distant building with the clock is Hawkins drapers shop, the only building that can be identified today; all the other buildings on the left were swept away in the development of the Aston University Campus in the 1970s. *C. C. Thornburn*

Above In Gosta Green, and carrying an advertisement for St Martin Chunky marmalade, is 40hp Brush-bodied car 687 of 1924. The elderly couple are in no rush to leave the tram as there is no other traffic. The tram will travel along Aston Road, passing on the right the Ionic-capitalled facade of the former Delicia cinema. This old picture house still remains as a reminder of the more bizarre architectural styles associated with the early years of the cinema. It has variously been a BBC television studio and an Arts Theatre for Aston University. Another reminder of the types of building that have been demolished is the distant terrace of three-storey 19th-century houses; these would be cleared in the 1960s. To the right of the Austin pick-up van is where the 7 tram route, the first to be abandoned in Birmingham, formerly went on its way, via Lister Street, to Nechells. *C. C. Thornburn*

Below The trams left Gosta Green and travelled along Aston Road before turning into the main A38 towards Aston Cross. An outward-bound MRCW-built car, No 638, is about to make that turn in front of the distant Charles Wade factory as it passes stationary car 654 of the same class; Wade's were constructional engineers whose Midland Iron Works premises were located in Aston Road at its junction with Corporation Street. No 654 is coming into the city from Short Heath and appears to be picking up a goodly number of passengers at the tram stop outside The Aston Junction builders' merchants on 17 November 1951. The tall building with the attic dormer windows is the long-demolished New Peacock public house. *R. B. Parr*

Above The junction of Aston Road and Dartmouth Street is today part of Dartmouth Circus, but on this sunny Monday 29 June 1953 it is still just another cobbled junction. Car 620 appears to be empty and is probably running into the city from Miller Street to undertake the duty to Barnabas Road, a shortworking of the 2 route that stopped halfway along Sutton New Road about a mile short of the actual terminus. The Austin KB8 Three-Way van is passing the Premier Garage, an Austin agency, yet the only two new vehicles visible in the showroom appear to be a Standard Vanguard Estate and a Land Rover! *T. J. Edgington*

Below Two boys roller-skate into Aston Road past the run-down Victorian terraces as car 639 reverses into Miller Street on 2 July 1953. This MRCW-bodied car is 40 years old and typical of the BCT fleet operated from Miller Street in the last year of tramcar operation. Some 121 trams were extant at the start of 1953 and, although overhauling had ceased in 1951, cars still went through the works for mechanical attention. All the survivors were the older all-electric cars with 40hp or 63hp motors. These were chosen, rather than the later air-braked, high-horsepower trams, because it was considered too expensive to retrain Miller Street depot drivers on the newer but unfamiliar tramcar types. *T. J. Edgington*

Above Built in 1911 as a standard BCT-style open-balconied UEC car, No 347 was rebuilt in July 1921 with a totally enclosed top deck and served as the prototype for all the subsequent new cars in the fleet. Totally enclosed four-wheel double-deck cars on narrow gauge systems were considered by the Board of Trade to be unstable on exposed lines because of the extra upper saloon weight, but the four-wheel shortcomings of No 347 were conveniently forgotten and it continued in service until September 1950. It stands opposite the entrance to Miller Street depot on 10 July 1949 on one of the ten sets of points that fanned into it. *A. N. H. Glover*

Below Cars 672, 679, 578 and 571 stand at the entrance to Miller Street depot, but time is running out for the trams as a replacement bus, a Crossley-bodied Daimler CVG6, stands among them. The Birmingham fleet of trams was not allowed to become run down even in the last days of operation, but there is a certain dismal lack of sparkle to these elderly, dignified cars as they await another day's work. Unfortunately car 571, which is attracting some attention at the far end of the row, has a broken axle and will not run on the final two days of operation. *R. F. Mack*

Above At Miller Street the main road became Aston Road North. UEC car 581, built in 1914, passes the wide throat at the junction of Miller Street and Aston Brook Street. As a couple wait to push their bicycles across the busy main road, the cars in the street are mainly prewar vehicles including a Morris Ten Series M, a Ford 7W Ten and a Standard Flying Ten. The tram is travelling towards Aston Cross on the 2 route to Erdington on 25 April 1953. The tall buildings behind it included a George Baines bakery shop, whose Handsworth-baked bread and cakes had a large following among people living on the north side of the city. *R. J. S. Wiseman*

Below Car 668 is in Aston Road North, which was all but swept away in the early 1970s with the opening of the Aston Expressway. The tram route was lined with small factories and workshops, but once the trams reached the distant Aston Cross the industrial landscape became dominated by the HP Sauce factory and Ansell's Brewery. This view of car 668 on the 78 route was taken from a following tram with, in the distance, another tram city-bound. Dominating the view is the 1882 bell tower of St Mary's Church. *H. B. Priestley*

On the afternoon of 22 June 1953, at 3.39pm, two trams, No 583 on the 2 route and 665 on the 79, are seen at Aston Cross on their way into the city. Although this urban scene, looking down Lichfield Road, seems to have an air of permanence, this is deceptive. The clock was not the original one, and the Ansell's Brewery had been built on the site of an old Georgian public house and would itself close in January 1981. The 30-year-old trams were already into their last two weeks of operation and would be replaced by Crossley, Daimler and Guy buses. Even the classic style of telephone box on the corner of Park Road is now all but phased out by British Telecom, as is the Belisha crossing, a 1930s device named after the then Minister of Transport, Leslie Hore-Belisha. *A. N. H. Glover*

Top Waiting at the tram stop railings beneath the Aston Cross clock of 1881, which replaced an earlier one, is MRCW car 647. It is working on the 78 service to Short Heath on 4 July 1953, almost its last run before being driven off to Witton depot for scrapping. The shops behind the tram were built in the 1840s and by this time not only included A. D. Wimbush, the baker, but also a Home & Colonial store, a George Mason grocery store and a row of shops belonging to the Birmingham Co-operative Society. In front of the tramcar is the huge Ansell's Brewery, developed throughout the 20th century until succumbing to closure in January 1981, 100 years after it was opened by Joseph Ansell. With the smell of malt and beer coming from Ansell's and the sharper odour of vinegar from the HP Sauce factory, Aston Cross was a place to make the mouth water. *C. Carter*

Middle Another view of Aston Cross, where the tram-loading barriers were used by all the Lichfield Road routes. This busy intersection had also been served by the 3X tram to Witton, which was abandoned on the last day of 1949; that route had followed the line of the buildings behind the clock tower. Car 721 is just manoeuvring over the crossover and its trolley-pole is already on the out-of-city wire; this in turn is delaying car 542 on its way to Erdington. This busy scene is on the last evening of operation when the Victorian suburb was still thriving and before urban renewal began to cater for cars rather than people. *T. J. Edgington*

Bottom Birmingham's last tramcar, No 616, is seen performing 'the last rites' on its final journey to Erdington, passing Ansell's Brewery at about 11.10am on Saturday 4 July 1953. The heavily laden tram is on its way from Aston Cross, which it has just left, and is going towards the Victoria Road junction, which is just beyond the brand-new MCCW-bodied Guy 'Arab' IV bus in the distance. Car 616 attracts some attention from the Ansell's workers and the pedestrians, as the passing of the tram also signifies the passing of an era. Note the pillion rider following the tram with wreath held aloft. *C. Carter*

Above During that final morning of operation, as the trams made the return trip to the city from the outer suburbs they were gradually taken out of service in Lichfield Road near Victoria Road, and passengers were transferred to waiting buses. Car 620, one of the 63hp Brush 62-seater cars of 1920, turns into Victoria Road from Lichfield Road with the legend 'Now 66 bus' chalked on its dash panel. This had been one of the last trams to work the 79 route from Pype Hayes Park, and is about to make the one-way trip to Witton depot, about 2 miles away. A total of 44 trams were broken up there in July 1953, and car 620 would be one of them. *A. N. H. Glover*

Below On that last Saturday the first tram to be replaced on the Aston Road routes was car 730, which was on an inward journey from Pype Hayes on the 79 route. Under the supervision of Traffic Inspectors, the tram passengers are being shepherded from the doomed tramcar to the spanking new bus. This vehicle is No 3026 (MOF 26), a 55-seater Guy 'Arab' IV with a Gardner 6LW engine. It is standing in Lichfield Road facing Victoria Road, with its driver receiving last-minute instructions through his open cab door. Travelling towards Aston station and Pype Hayes is car 691, working on one of the last 79 route trams out of the city. *Author's collection*

Above The former LNWR railway bridge across Lichfield Road at Aston was rebuilt on Sunday 25 March 1906 to accommodate, initially, CBT's open-top electric double-deck cars, but top-covered trams, such as the ubiquitous Radial 71 class cars and the even taller 'Aston' bogies numbered 1-20, were officially banned from passing beneath it. The two ex-CBT bogie cars 451 and 452 were used on the Erdington route in the late 1930s, but only prior to having new tyres fitted. However, the newer 'low-bridge' 301 class were, at 15ft 7½in, some 6 inches lower than the Radials and could just squeeze under the girders. Car 317 approaches the bridge along Lichfield Road near the Grosvenor Road junction on the left on its way to Stockland Green on a sunny day in 1914. An intrepid motorcyclist follows the tram, while a horse and a heavily loaded cart struggles up the cobbled road surface on the right. *Author's collection*

Below Even though the road beneath the bridge was subsequently lowered, it was always a tight squeeze to get a standard 15ft 6in top-covered tram under it. Strengthened Brush car 556 is about to pass beneath it on its way to Short Heath on the last morning of operation. To provide sufficient clearance, the overhead wires were at the side of the road so that the trams' trolley-poles were level with the car roof. The tram is being followed out of the city by an Austin Big 7 of 1939 vintage, while an Austin K4 lorry approaches the bridge, passing Holborn Hill on the extreme right, which led to Aston locomotive shed. *A. N. H. Glover*

Above Once beyond Aston Hall Road, Lichfield Road passed Salford Park and the junction with Cuckoo Road, where the tramway occupied a short 600-yard length of reserved track. Here No 625, one of the Brush-bodied 63hp cars, is working into the city on the 78 route from Short Heath. Although it is 1948, this car is still carrying the dignified, if somewhat shabby, fully lined-out prewar livery. Tram 625 was one of 354 bogie cars in Birmingham, all of which had maximum traction bogies; No 625 was built with Brush Burnley units whose outer 31½-inch driving wheels can be identified by the higher positioning of the axle-boxes. *F. Lloyd Jones*

Below Car 661, numerically the last of the MRCW cars of 1923, is working the 2 route from Erdington on 7 June 1953. It has just crossed Salford Bridge, opened in 1926 to carry Lichfield Road over the River Tame and the Birmingham & Fazeley Canal. The tram is just about to enter the short section of reserved track in Lichfield Road, which is protected by a pair of rather ornate bollards, one of which is visible in the foreground. The elderly flat-capped gentleman has time to sit on the bench on the left and watch the comings and goings at what was in 1953 a fairly busy stretch of road. Today he would soon be choked by exhaust fumes from the elevated M6 motorway at Gravelly Hill interchange; even Lichfield Road is today dominated by an almost never-ending traffic jam beneath the concrete motorway stilts. *J. H. Meredith*

Gravelly Hill to Erdington

As mentioned earlier, the junction at Salford Bridge at the bottom of Gravelly Hill was the point where the three main Aston Road routes split (see the map of page 95). The 2 route to Erdington, originally lettered 'E' until 1915, continued straight ahead and carried on through the busy and prosperous shopping centre of High Street, Erdington.

Increasing congestion led to the building of the Sutton New Road bypass in September 1938, and the trams were diverted on to this new reserved track route; this was the last section of new track opened in Birmingham. The last five-eighths of a mile of the route climbed Sutton Road, crossing Chester Road by passing through the middle of another traffic island, and reached the terminus latterly on a small piece of side reservation in the Edwardian shopping centre at the city boundary with Sutton Coldfield.

Above Brush car 692, working the 2 route from Erdington towards the city, is seen at Gravelly Hill on 22 June 1953 with its canvas sun-visor extended and carrying the typical St Martin Chunky marmalade and 'Say CWS and Save' advertisements. The wires to the right are the 79 route along Tyburn Road to Fort Dunlop and Pype Hayes; the Short Heath 78 route turned to the left of the tram shelters and into Slade Road. Car 692 is beginning to show signs of platform sag, something that even a few years earlier would have been unknown. *A. N. H. Glover*

Right Inbound car 647 negotiates the Gravelly Hill junction as it passes a somewhat disinterested and underemployed police officer on traffic duty. On a wet Wednesday 15 September 1937 the tram has just descended Gravelly Hill and is about to stop at the tram shelters just beyond the junction. It has been surmised that BCT had planned that all the Erdington routes were to close as the penultimate set of routes in 1943; however,

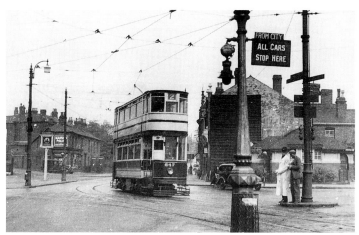

they were reprieved because of the ever-worsening state of public transport during the Second World War. As it transpired it was the newer, more complicated air brake cars running along the Bristol Road routes that were withdrawn in July 1952, a year before those to Erdington. *H. B. Priestley*

Above After the wide open spaces of Salford Bridge, the 2 route climbed up Gravelly Hill and on to the flatter but narrower road that led to the Six Ways, Erdington, junction. In this area the whole character of the route changed, becoming lined with large late-19th-century villas in their own grounds. This was something of a contrast with the houses just 2 miles further in towards the city. Car 653, one of the ubiquitous MRCW cars allocated to Miller Street depot, is working the 2 route and is just letting off a passenger at the Hunton Hill stop. The overtaking Austin Three-Way van of Marsh & Baxter takes up much of the remainder of the carriageway. *C. C. Thornburn*

Below Until 25 September 1938 the 2 route trams travelled along High Street, Erdington, which was one of the most important suburban shopping centres in Birmingham. After that date the last new section of tram route in Birmingham on the reserved track in Sutton New Road was brought into operation. On 10 July 1935, car 657, one of the 25 Midland RC&W tramcars, has just left the passenger loading railings that occupied the centre of the small traffic roundabout at Six Ways, Erdington – Birmingham's first, dating from 1926 – and travels along the High Street working on the 2 route. Archer's grocery store, with its plethora of period advertisements, stands on the corner of Summer Road, and was the only real casualty when work on the Erdington by-pass was begun in 1936. The new road was cut through roughly where the distant telegraph pole is located on the left. Just visible on the right is the Baptist Church on the corner of High Street and Wood End, built in 1878. Despite having been extended four times before the end of the Edwardian period, it was demolished in 1961, having closed three years earlier. *Birmingham Central Reference Library*

Above The Birmingham custom of allowing tramcars to go through the centre of an island did little to improve traffic flow, while actually having a tram stop in the middle of the island appears, by today's standards, to be at best bizarre and at worst dangerous! Brush-built car 608, one of nine of the class strengthened in 1948, leaves the tram stop on its way back to the city on the 2 route. On this sunny day in late June 1953 the majority of the windows are open, while the driver has obeyed the regulations and kept the lower saloon door shut. In the background Crossley DD42/7 bus No 2388 (JOJ 388), with a Crossley body, negotiates the island, working the famous 25-mile-long Outer Circle 11 route. *T. J. Edgington*

Below High Street, Erdington, remains much the same as when car 680 worked the 2 route through the suburb – the main difference is that Boots the Chemist was then a small shop, while today, like many of its multi-national contemporaries, it is a large multi-produce store. Car 680 was one of the 40 bogie tramcars ordered from Brush in 1924, and was one of eight of the 662 class to be destroyed during the air raid that severely damaged Miller Street depot on 9 April 1941. *W. A. Camwell*

Above Strengthened UEC car 558 of 1913 speeds along Sutton New Road beneath rather sagging overhead. This by-pass route was opened on 25 September 1938 and allowed the 2 route and its shortworking, the 64 to Barnabas Road, to work along the central reservation. Only the Ford Anglia appears to have any desire for speed, as the elderly gentleman saunters across the almost deserted carriageway. It is 29 June 1953 and car 558 has only a week left in service. *T. J. Edgington*

Below The 50th anniversary of the closure of the Birmingham tram services took place on Friday 4 July 2003. The author used his preserved former Birmingham City Transport Crossley DD42/6 No 2489 (JOJ 489) to recreate the first hours of the replacement bus services. The bus left the city centre at 10.48am, which was when tramcar 616 had left on the last ceremonial journey to Erdington in 1953. The bus started the tour from Colmore Circus, which was the nearest available point to the old Steelhouse Lane terminus. With the author at the wheel, the bus stands in Sutton New Road, suitably adorned with bus replacement notices, just beyond the distant junction with Summer Road, masquerading as the first 64 bus of 1953. It is standing almost opposite where tram 558 stood facing in the opposite direction in the previous photograph. It was a good day! *Diana Harvey*

Above In 1924 and 1925 Birmingham ordered 70 tramcars bodied by the Brush Company. Outwardly identical, the first 40 cars of the 662 class had Dick, Kerr DK30B 40hp motors, while the 702-731 class had GEC WT 32H 40hp motors. Cars 691 and 726, one of each of the two types, pass on the central reservation of Sutton New Road at Barnabas Road in 1953. Cars such as No 726 were considered sluggish compared with other classes working from Miller Street, but still amassed some 831,000 miles in the 28 years that they were in service. *C. C. Thornburn*

Below The tram route to Erdington was originally due to open on New Year's Day 1907, but because of the failure to agree terms to allow through running, the extension from Salford Bridge did not take place until 22 April 1907. The route initially used the early members of the second batch of open-topped four-wheel Brill cars, numbered 221-270, which had entered service between March and May 1907. Here UEC-built 35hp car 227, with its 'flop-over' destination boards incorrectly set, passes Slaney's boot shop at No 82, as it travels along High Street, Erdington, travelling from The Green on its way towards Six Ways in 1908. *Author's collection*

Despite its number – now associated with bad luck – tramcar 666, ordered from Brush in October 1923, survived until withdrawal in April 1953 with worn wheel flanges. Working on the 2 route to Erdington, it is loading up outside Shufflebotham's grocery stores on the corner of Wilton Road facing The Green in 1938. To the extreme left is ground in front of the Swan Inn public house, which in later years would take over Shufflebotham's premises to become its 'outdoor'. The bus is No 967 (COX 967), an almost new Leyland-bodied Leyland 'Titan' TD4c, which is working on the cross-city 17 service to Chester Road from the Maypole. Above the bus is the steeple of St Thomas and St Edmund Roman Catholic Church in Sutton Road; dating from 1848, it was seen as one of the best examples of High Victorian Gothic architecture. Behind the Armstrong-Siddeley car, at the back of The Green on the right, is the premises of Darrall's butchers shop, while in the older, two-storey building are the offices of Britannic Assurance. *W. A. Camwell*

Top After leaving Sutton New Road, the narrow uphill climb of High Street was reached. Briefly capturing the feel of the hamlet that once was Erdington, the Georgian tiled-roof cottages bear testimony to years of neglect. Car 664, devoid of advertisements, is passing Erdington Roman Catholic Church, built in the Decorated style in the mid-19th century. The entrance to the churchyard is at the lych-gate, which can be seen behind the trees. *F. Lloyd Jones*

Middle The third traffic roundabout through which tramcars passed on the Erdington route was at the Sutton Road/Chester Road junction. Here car 677, one of the usual 40hp Brush cars of the 662 class, has just left the terminus and the driver is looking out for traffic on the island before accelerating across Chester Road. The Edwardian shopping area around the road junction was always considered to be a somewhat superior part of north Birmingham: '...a dormitory borough of considerable charm with a cross section of all social groups in the population, but an unusually large percentage of well-to-do business and professional people.' (Municipal Review, 1955) Sutton Road continued beyond the city boundary to Sutton Coldfield. Although Sutton had plans for a tram service, it never materialised, and Midland Red took over the option on the route. However, double-decker buses were not allowed into Sutton until the Second World War, since it was thought by the local residents that they might intrude into the privacy of large residential buildings along the route. *S. J. Eades*

Bottom The terminus of the Erdington service was on a short length of side reserved track in Sutton Road. Car 693 has to wait for the tram at the terminus to leave before it goes into the single-line stub beside the distant shelter, and judging by the distant figures of the driver and conductor of the other tram, the crew have a considerable wait ahead of them. Few Birmingham bogie cars carried advertisements until after the Second World War, and when they did it tended to spoil their appearance. In this 1938 view, however, the 14-year-old Brush-bodied car has a number of dented panels and looks in need of a repaint. *Author's collection*

Above The original terminus of the tram service to Erdington was in Sutton Road opposite an Edwardian row of shops. These predated the opening of the tram service by just two years and included, uniquely in Birmingham, a waiting and refreshment room. The trams terminated just short of Harman Road on track in the middle of the road, where open-top UEC car 233 is loading up with a group of women on their way to the shops in Erdington. Although this tram received a top cover, it always retained its exposed platforms and was withdrawn as early as December 1930. *Commercial postcard*

Below The original terminus of the 2 route in Sutton Road was opposite where the tree is planted, but it was moved into the service road in front of the shops beyond Broadfields Road to help relieve congestion on the main A5127 road between Birmingham and Sutton Coldfield. The shops date from the 1920s and are therefore contemporary with the tram. Car 661, the last of the MRCW trams of 1923, belongs to the first class of new tramcars to be built with totally enclosed balconies. It is standing in the lay-by next to the Bundy Clock and the elaborate, if somewhat draughty, passenger shelter in 1952. In the distance are waiting Midland Red buses on services to Sutton Coldfield. Until 1938 the Royal Burgh of Sutton Coldfield would not allow double-deck buses into the town. *G. Morant*

Gravelly Hill to Short Heath

As with all the Aston Road group of routes, the route along Slade Road was worked from Miller Street depot. The original route was opened to Stockland Green and, when numbered in 1915, it was given the route number 1.

The route left the junction at Gravelly Hill and passed beneath the narrow former LNWR railway line to Sutton Coldfield and Lichfield. The section from the bridge to Stockland Green has perhaps changed least of all the Birmingham routes since abandonment, and still retains the feel of a prosperous, if somewhat older, residential area. The shops at Stockland Green marked the end of the route as first opened on 12 June 1912.

On 23 June 1926 the route was extended on reserved track into what was then virtually open country to serve the council estate under construction at Short Heath (see the map on page 95). Nearly 30 years after the abandonment the central reservation was rebuilt for the 'Trackline 65' experiments using the guided bus principle, which was in turn abandoned. Later, thankfully, new trees were planted to replace those planted in 1953.

Right Unlike the civic ceremony that took place on 22 April 1907 when the Erdington route opened, the Stockland Green service along Slade Road appears to have begun quietly on Sunday 12 June 1912. On leaving Salford Bridge the route turned left into a short, narrow section of road where UEC bogie car 581 is seen on 29 June 1953. The original Stockland Green service, numbered 1, became a shortworking of the extended 78 service to Short Heath on 23 June 1926. *T. J. Edgington*

Below The former LNWR Aston and Lichfield railway line passed over Slade Road by means of an attractively porticoed skewed bridge, from which tramcar 542 has just emerged. It is the last morning of operation on the 78 route as this 40-year-old tram travels towards Salford Bridge and the city centre. Two trams could pass each other under the bridge but they took up virtually all of the road space; pedestrians were given the added protection of steel barriers under the bridge on one side of the road. The green Morris Commercial lorry of the Public Works Department on the left is parked on the wrong side of the road, although its workmen are nowhere to be seen. They would soon be involved in the ancillary work of the abandonment as they removed items of street furniture and the last vestiges of the tramway system. Perhaps they were installing the traffic lights to control the narrow entrance to the bridge when the replacement buses were introduced. *A. N. H. Glover*

Above Seen from the other side of the bridge in late June 1953, car 580 is working the 78 route on its way to the city. This bridge marked a real change in the urban landscape on the Short Heath route as Edwardian terrace houses with small gardens and bay windows took over from the basically industrial landscape towards Salford Bridge. On this sunny afternoon, the 40hp UEC-built tram trundles along with only one more week to run in service. *T. J. Edgington*

Below Car 664 climbs up Slade Road past the terraced housing that lined most of the route to the original terminus at Stockland Green. Some distance behind the houses to the right lay the former LNWR railway station at Gravelly Hill, opened on 2 June 1863 on the line to Sutton Coldfield. This line encouraged the usual rapid urban growth, but left the short-haul journeys in need of street transport, which is why the tram routes benefited the local community and the short-distance passenger. *F. Lloyd Jones*

Above In the Erdington area in the early postwar years a number of what were called 'temporary bungalows' were built. As they were only 'temporary', the policy was to build them around the perimeters of open spaces such as parks and recreation grounds and not on sites designated for permanent future housing. Although the Birmingham Housing Department was initially against them, between 1945 and the end of the decade some 4,625 prefabricated dwellings had been built, including those in Slade Road near Highcroft Hospital's grounds. Brush-built bogie car 719 leaves the stop outside these 'prefabs' as a little boy sits on the steps to his still quite new house on 22 November 1952. For many of the new 'prefab' dwellers, life was a revelation with a fitted kitchen, indoor bathroom and toilet, two or three bedrooms and a garden. That they had a life expectancy of ten years didn't seem to matter, and although most were swept away in the 1960s, some still survive in Billesley as listed buildings; those seen here have been demolished and replaced by new single-storey brick-built homes. *R. B. Parr*

Below The electric tram route to Stockland Green was opened on 12 June 1912. This was the first available date when Miller Street depot had spare tramcar capacity, having returned its Handsworth services to Hockley depot after the latter was finally converted from cable car operation. The route to Stockland Green was initially operated by Brill open-toppers, but within a year was being operated by cars from the first third of the 301 class cars. Car 327 pulls away from the tram stop in a cloud of dust in Slade Road near Stockland Green terminus in about 1913, while the two mothers pushing prams seem oblivious to the 12½-ton tram bearing down on them. *Commercial postcard*

The original terminus at Stockland Green was typical of pre-First World War examples in Birmingham, consisting of a late-19th/early-20th-century shopping area at an important road junction. However, the extension of the tram route to Short Heath reduced the original terminus to just another shopping centre on the route. On 1 July 1953, the last Wednesday before closure, car 608 prepares to return to Miller Street under the anonymous destination 'Depot Only'. *G. F. Douglas*

Right This view of Stockland Green, looking out of the city a few days earlier on 29 June 1953, reveals the opening up of the road beyond Marsh Hill. The large building in the background is the Plaza cinema, opened on Boxing Day 1927. Coincidentally, two other large suburban cinemas, the Robin Hood at Hall Green and the Crown in Icknield Port Road, were also opened on the same day. Car 713, one of the GEC-motored, Brush-built trams, stands at the old terminus, seemingly unsure whether it is a 59 shortworking to Gravelly Hill or a 78 going to the city; it was, however, common practice to leave different shortworking destinations on the blinds so they did not have to be

changed by the conductor. The Typhoo Tea advertisement, claiming it to be 'One of the good things of life', replaced the more contentious one claiming that tea aided digestion. One wonders if the crew of the tram had one of those white enamel pots that were standard BCT platform staff issue? If so, was it filled with Typhoo tea, brewed up for them in The Snack Bar? Or were the 'Delicious Ices' too much of a temptation? *T. J. Edgington*

Below Car 657 crosses the junction with Marsh Lane and enters the 1-mile-long reserved track to Short Heath. This extension from Stockland Green along Streetly Road was opened as the 78 service on 23 June 1926, and the MRCW-bodied tram is working empty from the depot to

the terminus on 9 May 1953. On the left is the wall of the mock-Jacobean Stockland Inn, opened on 24 November 1924 by M&B on the corner of Marsh Hill on the site of Stockland Green Farm, which had been a genuine 18th-century farmhouse. On the extreme right is the Plaza cinema, which opened with the silent film *The Cat and the Canary* starring Laura La Plante, and closed to become a bingo hall at the end of September 1978. Next door, where the van is parked on the pavement, was the vital necessity of the night out – the local fish and chip shop. When the pub, the tram route and the cinema were first opened, the housing estate was barely under way, although in nearby Ilford Road, at the end of 1925, a new house would cost £375 6s. *H. B. Priestley, National Tramway Museum*

Top The Streetly Road tram extension from Stockland Green was opened on 23 June 1926 to serve a large new council house development. Former open-balconied Brush car 636, which had been totally enclosed in November 1931 at Kyotts Lake Road Works, has just left the terminus of the 78 route on 7 June 1953. By this time the state of the track left something to be desired and the rapid acceleration of the cars down the hill caused a considerable amount of 'hunting', or 'tail-wagging', even with these bogie cars. The central reservation was typical of the later Birmingham tram route extensions, being tree-lined, fairly straight and designed for high-speed running. *J. H. Meredith*

Middle The terminus was approached by a climb up the reserved track to Short Heath Road. The intention had been to extend the route into the Banners Gate estates and New Oscott, but this was outside the then city boundary so the route was never developed, although tantalisingly, beyond the terminus, the road continues as a brief length of dual carriageway. Leaving the row of shops at the Short Heath terminus on 6 June 1953 is Brush totally enclosed bogie car 664, while on the left is UEC car 549, which had entered service in the early months of 1914. *L. W. Perkins*

Bottom Car 645 stands at the substantial shelters at the Short Heath terminus in the spring of 1953, having evidently just arrived as its trolley-pole has not been turned for the return journey to the city centre. The driver's end of the tram is parked opposite the Bundy Clock so that the driver could 'peg the clock' prior to leaving the terminus. The later reserved track extensions were well laid out and it was a pity that, once the last major extensions had been built in the late 1920s, the lead that Birmingham Corporation had built up in tramway development was allowed to stagnate. The intention had been to extend the service to Banners Gate at the entrance to Sutton Park, but this never took place. This could have been the equivalent of the Lickey Hills, but on the north side of the city. *C. Carter*

Gravelly Heath to Pype Hayes and Fort Dunlop

At Gravelly Hill the 79 route turned right into Tyburn Road, which had been built with help from the Dunlop Tyre Company. Since the end of the First World War Dunlop had used a passenger barge to ferry its workers from the tram terminus at Salford Bridge along the Birmingham & Fazeley Canal to the factory at Fort Dunlop. The route was opened on reserved track as far as Holly Lane on 13 May 1920 and extended along Holly Lane to the gates of Fort Dunlop on 13 February 1930. This was the last route extension in Birmingham and, unusually,

was opened by ex-Company car 472, which was fully decorated for the ceremony.

Originally the route along Tyburn Road was at the side of the road, but it became the central reservation some years later when the second, northern, carriageway was constructed. Tyburn Road was unusual in that it marked the boundary between residential and industrial landscapes. The latter occupied the River Rea side of the valley and the council housing the northern side.

Some way beyond Bromford Lane, where, after 1926, the Outer Circle bus service crossed the tram route, was the bus repair works. Just beyond was the Fort Dunlop

Right Once into Tyburn Road, having turned right from Gravelly Hill, the first crossover was used by the 5 route, as this was its eastern terminus. Car 539, one of the 1914 UEC bogie cars that had been delivered as an open-balconied tram, is about to turn back to Lozells. It is waiting for a city-bound 79 tram, which has just travelled the length of Tyburn Road and will turn left to the tram shelters at Salford Bridge, just before reaching Gravelly Hill. This tram is one of the Brush-bodied 42hp vehicles built on EMB Burnley-type bogies. Today on the right is the elevated section of the M6, with its incessant roar of traffic, but the Tame Valley of 1953 was only followed by the Birmingham & Fazeley Canal. A reminder of the barge traffic is the sign, alongside Salford Bridge Wharf, for Spencer Abbott & Co, canal boat builders. *Author's collection*

Right The first intersection along Tyburn Road was at Bromford Lane, where the Outer Circle bus route crossed on its way from The Fox and Goose on the right to Six Ways, Erdington, on the left; alongside this junction was the Navigation public house, which stood alongside the Birmingham & Fazeley Canal. Built in the late 1920s, not long after Tyburn Road had been opened, the Bromford Lane junction was made into a tram 'drive-through' traffic island in about 1934. On 14 April 1938 car 663, one of the Brush bogie cars of 1924, travels through the island towards the city on the 79 service. The concept of putting the tram stop and shelter on the island was not perpetuated when vehicular traffic flows increased. Meanwhile at the Apollo cinema, further along Tyburn Road, George Arliss, famous for his portrayal of Benjamin Disraeli, is starring, melodramatically, in *Doctor Syn*. *H. B. Priestley, National Tramway Museum*

turning into Holly Lane, and another hundred yards or so further was the junction with Kingsbury Road.

Below The reserved track along Tyburn Road was partly financed by Dunlop and, until the municipal housing development began, it ran through open country to the factory. Here car 580 demonstrates both the advantages and disadvantages of reserved track operation: the trams were certainly separated from the traffic – although in this 4 May 1953 view there is parlously little need for such

The route was extended by about three-quarters of a mile to Chester Road at Pype Hayes Park as the 79 route on 20 February 1927.

separation – but the main difficulty was that passengers had to cross the road in order to reach the tram stop. Behind the trees on the right is the large bus repair works opened in 1929 and closed early in 1933. It is one of the ironies of the BCT system that after 1937, when the Stratford Road routes closed, the bus repair works was on a tram route and the tram repair works was on a bus route! *C. C. Thornburn*

Below UEC-built tram 571 slowly reverses across the tracks near the original Tyburn Road terminus at Holly Lane on 30 June 1953. Tyburn Road is unusual in that the north-west side is 1920s municipal housing and the south-east side consists of factory units occupying the land on the terraces above the River Tame. The lowest land, nearest the river, was used largely in connection with the purification of sewage, although above the flood plain were numerous larger factory units such as Fort Dunlop and the Fisher & Ludlow car body factory. The factories that actually lined Tyburn Road, as can be seen behind the tram, were much smaller units often doing the sort of engineering that gave the city its famous industrial heritage. *T. J. Edgington*

Above The Fort Dunlop siding was opened on 13 February 1930 when suitably decorated car 472 carried civic dignitaries back to the city centre having broken a ceremonial tape in Holly Lane. This was the penultimate tramway extension in Birmingham and was used for short workings by both the 5 service and as a new route into the city by way of Tyburn Road as the 63 route. Holly Lane was a private road belonging to the Dunlop Rubber Company, and was impressive with kerbside loading and manicured gardens and lawns reminiscent of the Cadbury chocolate factory grounds at Bournville. Car 726 waits just below the crest of the Birmingham & Fazeley Canal bridge with the impressive First World War factory in the background, while the crew of 688 wait to take their tram back to the Steelhouse Lane terminus in the city centre. *A. N. H. Glover*

Below On a sunny afternoon, 20 June 1953, Brush-built 63-seater car 716, equipped with EMB Burnley bogies and the rather slow Dick, Kerr DK30/1L 40hp motors, stands at the tram shelters in Holly Lane. The impressive Fort Dunlop proclaims the name of the Belfast veterinarian who invented the pneumatic tyre in 1888, although he was bought out by other entrepreneurs, such as E. T. Hooley, as early as 1895. By 1915 a 260-acre site had been chosen in open countryside in the Tame Valley and here Fort Dunlop was built, the somewhat military tower of which dominates the skyline. Behind the tram is 1950 MCCW-bodied Daimler CVD6 2029 (JOJ 29), the penultimate exposed-radiator Daimler bus supplied to BCT. These were probably the quietest and most refined of all Birmingham's postwar half-cab double-deckers. *T. J. Edgington*

Above About to leave the reserved track on Tyburn Road at Kingsbury Road is UEC car 579. As can be seen, the bulkhead platform window has been plated over, revealing this to be one of the strengthened 40hp cars, rebuilt in this form in December 1948 with EMB bogies and DK30B motors. In retrospect, it seems a lot of capital expenditure for only 4½ years of further service. The maintenance on the reserved track, with the encroaching weeds, seems to be becoming a little neglected by this date, as does the tram itself. *C. C. Thornburn*

Left MRCW-bodied tram 644 of 1923 is seen shortly after leaving the terminus at Pype Hayes on the 79 route. The council housing was developed throughout the outer suburbs of the city in the interwar period, the Pype Hayes development containing 1,344 houses, but ranking only 12th of 15 major housing schemes built between the wars. Some of the houses can be seen on the right-hand side of this view of Tyburn Road, taken in 1948. Car 644 was involved in an accident in December 1952 and was sold to W. T. Bird of Stratford-upon-Avon. This company was given the task of breaking up all the trams after 1950 and was well known for its scrapyard, which also contained many of Birmingham's former bus fleet. *F. Lloyd Jones*

Above The driver and conductor of Brush-bodied car 672 stand with their trusty tram at the Pype Hayes terminus on 17 May 1953. They look at both the car and the photographer with a slightly bemused expression, perhaps wondering why anyone would want to photograph their 41-year-old tram. The 79 route was opened on 20 February 1927 from Holly Lane to Pype Hayes to serve the small-windowed world of the council house estate. Behind the speeding Ford V8 Pilot is the Bagot Arms, typical of the huge public houses built at this period on these interwar housing estates. *A. N. H. Glover*

Below Despite all the contractual problems with their construction and delivery, the MRCW cars proved to be a very sound investment for BCT, and only six of the 637-661 class failed to see service over the last few days of operation. Car 657 is seen here alongside the distinctive wooden shelters erected at the end of the reserved track routes, with the entrance to Pype Hayes Park beyond the trees on the other side of Chester Road. *G. Wood*

INDEX OF LOCATIONS